Praise for Anne Seisen Saunders and
Full Circle:
Dharma Talks on Collective Awakening

Seisen Saunders is one of the most well rounded human beings that I have met. As well as a long and varied zen practice, including 20 years with Maezumi Roshi, being Treasurer and administrator of ZCLA, co-abbot of Yokoji ZenMountain Center. Founder and Abbot of Sweetwater Zen Center in San Diego. She is versed in Council and therapy practice, prison work and social action. This book exposes the myth of Buddhism being a quietistic approach to living, and is full of examples of active practice in the midst of daily life and in interesting situations. It is full of Seisen's unique common sense teaching and humor.

I wholeheartedly recommend this book.

— Charles Tenshin Fletcher,
Roshi, Abbot Yokoji Zen Mountain Center

FULL
CIRCLE

FULL CIRCLE

DHARMA TALKS ON COLLECTIVE AWAKENING

Anne Seisen Saunders

Edited by Bobby Chowa Werner

Copyright © 2025 by Anne Seisen Saunders

All rights reserved. No parts of this publication may be reproduced, distributed, or transmitted in any form or by any means, including photocopying, recording, digital scanning, or other electronic or mechanical methods, without the prior written permission of the publisher, except in the case of brief quotations embodied in critical reviews and certain other noncommercial uses permitted by copyright law.

Published by Madrona Arts Press
For permission requests, please contact: Diana.hartel@gmail.com

Edited by Bobby Chowa Werner
Book Design: Second Star Publishing Works

ISBN (paperback): 978-1-7327890-3-6
ISBN (ebook): 978-1-7327890-4-3

Library of Congress Control Number: 2024925911

ACKNOWLEDGMENTS

A big thank you to Bobby Chowa Werner, Sensei for helping to craft and edit this book. And to Diana Kosei Hartel for overseeing the publication process. And to Valerie Kyoshin Velez, Preceptor, Christopher Shoyu Cather, Margy Jisho Brookes, Tabitha Garrett, Catherine Rogers, and Paul Lewis Morgan. This book would not have happened without you.

TABLE OF CONTENTS

Foreword: Anne Seisen Saunders, Roshi	xiii
The Three Principles of Buddhism	1
Dreamy Peonies	13
Manifesting the Three Treasures	19
Circle Structure as the Three Treasures	27
The Sangha Sutra	35
The Bath Path I	43
This, That & Neither	51
Two Ends to Suffering	59
The Delusion of Practice	67
Effort & Mirror I	75
Effort & Mirror II	85
Your Ingredients I	89
Your Ingredients II	101
Precept Beings	113
The Bath Path II	119
Every Day Is True Nature	129
Picnic Zen	135
On Relationship I	145
On Relationship II	155
On Relationship III	161
Notes	165

*This work is dedicated to my teachers
Taizan Maeazumi, Roshi and Bernie Tetsugen Glassman,
Roshi, and also to The Sangha.*

FOREWORD

By Anne Seisen Saunders, Roshi

We are living in a fractured world. We apply a judgmental mind to every aspect of our life. More and more, we are separating ourselves into different tribes based on ideas that we have about the world. We are increasingly intolerant of those with different values and philosophies.

Most spiritual practices guide us to the direct experience of seeing everything as one body. The talks in this collection are an attempt to share ways to realize and actualize this truth. At Sweetwater Zen Center, we practice zazen and do koan study to realize the oneness of all things. We also practice Council as a way to experience group connection. We study the Precepts and use collective, compassionate policy making (see "The Sangha Sutra") as guides to the actualization of shared awakening.

FULL CIRCLE

My teacher Bernie Glassman was once asked, "How do you know a person is enlightened?" He Answered, "You can tell an enlightened person by how they live their life, and how they serve others." I'd like to share a story, to best demonstrate how collective awakening works. This is a true experience that a friend has shared with me.

THE COLD CHAIN BUS
by Paul Lewis Morgan,
PRISONER # 110562810

This is one of the most incredible experiences I've ever had in my life. I found myself in an odd position once, riding on a chain bus. A chain bus is basically how you're transported when you're incarcerated for things you may or may not have done. It's a chain bus because when you're incarcerated and you are transported to another unit, they chain you together. Usually, your wrist is handcuffed to another man's wrist, and you have to deal with that. Often times, the men who are chained together talk during the long ride and get to know each other on a deep level. But we were fortunate in this particular instance, (God bless Covid), that they could not chain us together.

This particular morning, we were called up to be moved from one place to another, and it was the

FOREWORD

coldest day that I've ever experienced. The temperature was below freezing. There were six of us—three black men, two Mexican men, and me, the white guy. We found ourselves being transported 300 miles to another unit for whatever reason. When you leave one facility to go to another, they take away your jackets and all the stuff that you're supposed to have to keep you warm, under the pretense that the bus is heated. The warm clothing belongs to the facility, so it is taken away before you get on the bus, and you are issued jackets again when you get to your next unit.

About three miles into our trip, we started yelling at the bus driver, "Boss, we need to turn on the heater. It's colder than a wells digger's ass!" But the boss said, "Sorry, maintenance couldn't fix it." So, as we all sat there looking around, freezing, this white boy went over and started banging on the heater. And lo and behold, because things are beautiful, a little heat started to come out. So, I was the first one to be able to enjoy that heat, as minimal as it was. Then I looked over at my friends and said, "Gentlemen, do any of you have any objections to getting a lot closer?" And before you knew it, everybody let their guard down. They separated themselves from the differences they imagined in their head. And they just said, "What do you want us to do?" And I said, "We should all just come here and form a little circle, and use what body heat we have left. And we could just kind of cuddle up, you know?"

Then all of a sudden, because it was so cold, we all huddled together around this little heater, and we wrapped our arms around each other and we just, we just stayed there. We rode it out. It was a beautiful thing. And when we got to where we were going, they gave us jackets and we were all like, "Yay, we made it! It was so cold, but aren't we so happy that we had each other to get through it?" It was one of the most beautiful things that ever happened to me in a world of confusion.

So, for anybody out there that's reading this, I highly, highly recommend that we all come together and share the warmth from our own hearts, especially in times when it seems so cold in the world. Remember that we're all in this together. End of story.

As time went on, all six of us that were on that bus have ended up seeing each other in different times in different places. And we've always embraced each other with hugs and gratitude for the warmth we shared during the coldest of times.

FOREWORD

I love this story so much. And I hope that the following collection of talks will help you be the best cold day chain bus rider you can be. To me, that's the *Bodhisattva Vow*—to serve all beings with the warmth from our own hearts.

THE THREE PRINCIPLES OF BUDDHISM

Thank you so much for your practice. I really appreciate it. Now I'll show you the picture I brought for today's talk. You are going to love this.

This is a picture from one of those super telescopes, and each of those itty-bitty shiny dots is a galaxy. And this is just one tiny cross-sectional view into the universe. Each galaxy has something like one hundred billion stars. And each star has at least one planet. So that's hundreds of billions of planets in each galaxy. And here on earth, there are 8 billion people.

That's our situation. That's who we are. I'm just one little person of 8 billion, on a planet that's one of a hundred billion planets in our galaxy. It's unfathomable. The guy who originally posted this picture on my feed said, "See how insignificant we are?" And people got really angry. "I'm not insignificant. I'm really important." So, who are we? What are we?

I was going through some old files, and I found this one called "Dharma Pith." And in it, I found an old note that Maezumi Roshi wrote up for me. One notable thing is that he wrote it on the United States Navy note paper, which I'm guessing is because Barry Kaigen McMahon, who was studying with Maezumi Roshi at the time, had been in the Navy.

I hardly have anything that Roshi wrote. And I can hardly remember that he wrote this for me, but it was probably at the end of my formal study. It says:

THE THREE PRINCIPLES OF BUDDHISM

[The Three Principles of Buddhism]
by Jyōkō-rōshi (a teacher of Kōyū-rōshi)

1. Maha-prajnya-paramita is the primary meaning of Buddhism. Contemplate it deeply from the bottom of your mind.

2. Three studies of the precepts, samadhi and wisdom are the key to attaining the Buddha Way. Maintain it diligently from the bottom of your mind.

3. The four vast vows are our original vows. Practice them reverently from the bottom of your mind.

THE THREE PRINCIPLES OF BUDDHISM

1. Maha Prajnaparamita is the primary meaning of Buddhism. Contemplate it deeply from the bottom of your mind.

2. Three Studies of the Precepts, samadhi, and wisdom are the key to attaining the Buddha Way. Maintain it diligently from the bottom of your mind.

3. The Four Vast Vows are our original vows. Practice them reverently from the bottom of your mind.

Every time I read this, I see something new. I love calling them "original vows." We chant them every day, sometimes a couple times a day.

In that same folder, there's something from the Bowen Family Systems, which elder Bob studied. Elder Bob was originally a clinical psychologist or psychiatrist. But then he studied therapy later on. And he studied the Bowen Family Systems. What I wrote down on this document is, "Self-observation is not self-blame." Dogen Zenji said, "To study the Buddha Way is to study the self." Intensive practice, like sesshin, is essentially study-the-self time. And sometimes we get to see things we wouldn't have expected. We see our failures, our errors, how we harm ourselves and others. And that's so good. But, "Self-observation is not self-blame." As these things come up, it's easy to fall into a very negative space. It's discouraging to truly see how our own greed, anger, and ignorance are at the root of suffering. But it goes against the Precepts to hate ourself, to judge ourself. Studying our self in zazen, we don't hold on to our ideas about ourself, we are able to "forget the self." And then we're free from blame.

Another thing I found in this folder is entitled *Perverted Views*. "Perverted views are attempting to seek permanence in what is essentially impermanent." And that goes back to Maha Prajnaparamita, the first of these Three Principles Maezumi Roshi wrote. Maha Prajnaparamita is Not-Knowing, emptiness, constant change. To try to make anything permanent is a perverted view, because the nature of our life is constant change. "Another perverted view is to see ease in what is suffering." Boy, do I do that: "Everything's cool. It's fine that people are trying to kill each other all over the world. All of the terrible suffering in the world is fine. Just have another joint, another glass of wine." The first New Year's Eve I ever did at ZCLA was in 1975, maybe '76. I was so unhappy, because I like a party. I still do. I like to anesthetize myself and forget about the suffering of the world. I don't say that's a *bad* thing to do, but I think it's very beneficial to be more intentional and sit with sangha on New Year's Eve.

Our practice is about facing reality, facing our true nature. As the first Noble Truth says, *life is suffering*. And there's an end to that suffering—deeply accepting that everything's constantly changing. To ignore the suffering of the world is a perverted view. To attach to selfhood is a perverted view. That's why I think people might feel angry when looking at a picture of the universe. It is overwhelming to face the reality of our relative smallness and impermanence. My needs, my desires, my opinions are so infinitesimally small in the context of the universe. Hanging onto them causes suffering, because hanging on is misaligned with the nature of the universe. Trying to create a selfhood, which wants to win and be the best, wants to get the award, comes out of a perverted view. Our true nature is no-self. That's Maha Prajnaparamita, no-self.

How grand is that?! If you wake up to no-self, then what are you? Look at this picture of space again. That's what you are. Just multiply that by billions upon billions. As Dr. Sagan posited of galaxies, stars, beings and landscapes—that's what you are, that's your true nature. But we can't truly see that as long as we hold onto our little ideas about our self.

Turning back to the Three Principles of Buddhism, it says, "Maha Prajnaparamita is the primary meaning." That is emptiness, no-self, oneness, the interconnection of absolutely everything. What am I? I am the whole universe. What is my true nature? Constantly changing. To memorize that as a statement, to know it intellectually, is nice. But our practice is about viscerally coming face-to-face with that truth, as Roshi said, from the bottom of our mind. And the best way to do that, in my opinion, is zazen. Of course, there are many spiritual practices. But to practice like this, doing lots and lots of zazen together, is an excellent path to realizing Maha Prajnaparamita.

The next Principle is about study. The order he uses is interesting: the Precepts, *samadhi* and wisdom. I tend to think of *samadhi* first. When you realize no-self, when body and mind really drop off, that experience is *samadhi*. To fully let go and be free of all the pain and suffering that comes with the sense of self—all the struggles around being the best and getting what I want, being right and judging everything—feels great. And that *samadhi* comes out of zazen.

Wisdom is seeing into the differences that come out of emptiness. It's seeing things as they are and understanding their uniqueness. The billions and billions of stars, the planets and people—each one is unique. I don't know if there's anything that isn't unique. And to become intimate with all of the phenomena of our life is the wisdom. We can discern what is repulsive, as the

THE THREE PRINCIPLES OF BUDDHISM

Perverted Views piece said. To delight in what is repulsive is not wisdom. The way we romanticize war in this country is not wisdom. Wisdom is to see the repulsive as it is—repulsive. It's to see suffering as suffering, and name it as such.

And then the Precepts help us cultivate this wisdom. We have an experience of oneness through our zazen practice, we get it in our gut. Then we're better able to develop wisdom, discerning what is compassion and what is "repulsive." And then, we ceaselessly struggle because we always have our greed, anger, and ignorance. All of us have those yelling at us all the time. So, the Precepts guide our path of living a life of *samadhi* and wisdom, as our little self keeps yelling at us.

The thing that really interested me was that the third principle is the Four Bodhisattva Vows. I don't know that I'd thought too much about these vows. We chant them all the time, though I usually just do it by rote. These "original vows" are something we're born with. They're not an idea or theory that's put upon us. And yet, we go on delighting in suffering and what is repulsive, and we ignore these innate vows.

The first of these vows is, "Beings are boundless, we vow to serve." Beings throughout the universe are literally boundless, infinite. And we vow as Bodhisattvas to serve others, to raise others up, above ourselves. But the "serving" in this vow is primarily to help all beings wake up to the oneness, the emptiness of everything. Out of that awakening comes wisdom and compassion, the Precepts and *samadhi*. And of course, as Bernie would say, for people who are hungry, who don't have housing, who are oppressed, it's very hard to practice. So, serving also includes promoting conditions in which all beings can have the safety and stability to be able to practice and realize no-self.

The second vow is, "Delusion is inexhaustible, we vow to transform." The point is not to get rid of delusion. Trying to do that doesn't work. But deluded karma, or energy, can transform through the practice of opening up and facing our delusion. Greed becomes abundance. So, open up to your greed: "I need a Mercedes-Benz so badly! Just a Mercedes Benz, and a color TV, and a good-looking guy. That's all I want, and then I'll be happy." Then open up to how painful it is to live with that greed. And as we sit in it, we notice that that pain naturally becomes appreciation. Whatever energy comes up, be it. Be that energy and get to know it. That greed energy is considered to be in the center of our body, the second *chakra*. Get to know that greed, and it will transform into abundance. There's enough for everybody. We already have everything.

There seem to be two greeds in the Five Buddha Families. One is the greed for stuff—Mercedes-Benz, and the color tv. The other is interpersonal greed, lust, needing somebody, that need for love, for sex. It's so powerful. That energy is in the first *chakra*, and it transforms into love and compassion for all beings. We can wake up to the fact that there's love everywhere, including within ourselves. Transform neediness into compassion.

Fear, or envy, feeling immobilized, they transform into action, loving action. We tend to have a fear that says, "If I really live for the sake of all beings, then I'll be hurt." There's that movie where a priest knows about child abuse in his church. But he feels like he can't say anything. In confession he says, "What can I do? I know what you say I should do, I should act. But if I do, maybe I'll be crucified." That's the fear involved in acting righteously. I've got that big time. But that fear can transform into loving action. And some of our greatest heroes have been able to transform fear into action for the sake of others. Then there's the delusion of denial, ignorance. Seeing ease in suffering and delighting in what is repulsive is denial. And it can transform into pure awareness of everything as it is.

Judgment is how we keep ourselves separate from others, as we hold on tightly to our little self. Gosh, I do this all the time. That's why I know it so well. But, sitting deeply with our judgment, it can transform into wisdom—seeing things as they are, independent of my conditioning and karma. Of course, our judgment allows us to discern when things are causing harm and are truly wrong. One of the Precepts is about not speaking of others' errors and faults, which is generally a good idea. But sometimes, we have to call people out. "What that person is doing is harming others, and something should be done about it. They shouldn't be allowed to continue in this way." Delusion is inexhaustible, we vow to transform.

The next original Bodhisattva vow says, "Dharma gates are everywhere, we vow to enter." Right now, in this moment, there are Dharma gates to the right, to the left, in front, in back, on top and below. These Dharma gates open to the realization of the perfection of this moment. Even in the worst times, they're all there. Sometimes they're very, very hard to access. But they're always here. That's where we have to have a little faith. Every moment is an entry place to no-self, to pure *samadhi*.

The last vow says, "Awakening is unsurpassable, we vow to practice." Bernie prefers "manifest." "Awakening is unsurpassable, we vow to manifest." But we decided "practice", partly because that's a closer translation. Sensei, Jitsujo Gauthier helped us with the translation, since she knows Chinese.

Can anyone just completely one hundred percent be aligned with these vows all the time? I doubt it. I'm certain I can't. But what I can do is continue to practice. As soon as I catch my delusion in action, I look at it, become it, sit with it every day, transform it, and then repeat these vows.

It's almost New Year's Eve. This time of year, we tend to make vows, which is a good thing. It's also a good thing to renew our vows every single day. We also renew the Precept vows every month. And these Bodhisattva vows, which Maezumi Roshi calls our original vows, don't necessarily have to be Buddhist. We practice them in this particular form, but just as every single person is unique, everyone's practice path is unique. You may have personal vows that look a little different, but they may resemble the essence of these innate vows that we all share.

We must pay attention to our karmic conditions and take care of our karmic needs. We can't deny them. Are there things you really want to do that you haven't done yet? For me, I need to take this time to learn Spanish. Every year I put it off; maybe this will be the year. But let's take some serious time to reflect on our original vows, our practice vows, our Bodhisattva vows, and also our karmic vows, our life vows. What is it that's calling to me? What do I really need to listen to?

Again, thank you so much for your practice. It's a hard time of year to sit hard, because the whole world is busy going into a little denial party time. But we're here making the effort to reflect and be aware, to transform. I encourage you to appreciate that. And I really encourage you to realize Maha Prajnaparamita, no-self. All of this just falls out of that. And taking care of it is tough. So, I thank you. I encourage you. Let's just keep on going.

DREAMY PEONIES

Today I want to talk about one of my favorite koans, which is actually in two of our koan collections. It's in the *Blue Cliff Record*, and it's in the *Book of Equanimity*.

> *Attention! Riko Taifu on one occasion asked Master Nansen, "Dharma Master Jo is exceedingly wonderful. He said, 'Heaven and earth have the same root. The 10,000 things are one body.'" Nansen, pointed to the peony in the garden and said, "Taifu, people nowadays see these flowers as if in a dream."*

I just recently said to someone during a casual chat, "We're all one." Something like that. And she said, "Oh, how trite can you get?" And I appreciated that. It's kind of nice to think that oneness is considered trite, now that it's so familiar in our culture.

"Heaven and earth have the same root. The 10,000 things are one body." We are not separate. But talking about it like that is kind of heady. If we look at Buddha's last teaching—the Eight Awarenesses of the Enlightened Person—he talks about how to avoid hollow discussion. In-depth discussion about ideas and concepts of what Buddhism teaches, what does that do? What is felt? How does that manifest? I read somewhere that the Buddha only ever explained his teaching once. Otherwise, there were no explanations, no treatise. The Buddha Way must be experienced.

That's what's so powerful about koans and sutras—getting in touch with these great masters who are able to directly express the oneness, non-dualism. It is a nearly impossible feat, because language is, by nature, dualistic. As soon as I open my mouth, I'm caught up in a dualistic idea. The first Pure Precept says: Don't Do Evil. Evil is defined as the act of separating. Don't separate. Ultimately, you actually can't separate anything, because the nature of our universe is non-dual. We just think we can separate and categorize things. So, separation is evil because it goes against the essential nature of our life.

Heaven and earth, same root. The spiritual and the common, same root. The 10,000 things are one body. It's easy to say all this, but to live that kind of love and connection takes constant effort, constant practice. So, my point is—it's a pretty heady thing to say to your teacher. It's kind of a hollow discussion. And so, Nansen, his teacher, points to a peony and says, "People nowadays see this peony as if in a dream."

I hate giving Dharma talks. I'm not kidding. I really hate it because you can't tell the truth. Whatever I say, I'm trying to express the ineffable with words and concepts. It just doesn't work. After every Dharma talk I give, I regret at least one thing I said. Even though it felt perfectly authentic and true at the time. I'm always worried, "Oh, I made this sound too stinky. I forgot to mention that aspect. People are going to misunderstand." I immediately want to send an email to everyone, "I didn't really mean that, I meant this." But then of course, even the fixing statement would invariably miss the mark. You just can't tell the full truth in a Dharma talk.

And that's why Nansen's reply is such a beautiful expression. "People nowadays see this peony as if in a dream." The Japanese love peonies. They have a peony festival. I think I was there once when they were in bloom. Or maybe I just saw it on TV. But it is beautiful, and the Japanese are absolutely crazy about them. We love flowers. They're so beautiful. Here where I live, as I look out the window, there's a carpet of wildflowers growing through my community. It's literally a carpet. And with these wildflowers came the worst hay fever I've ever had. My head hurts so bad and I'm constantly sneezing. And now they're starting to wilt, they're dying. They all have to be cut down soon, because they become a fire hazard.

Notice all the thoughts and ideas that come up around seeing a beautiful flower—I wish I had flowers like that in my garden; spring and flowers are the best thing in the world; ohhh, my hay fever. A slew of complex emotions, memories, and associations arise with this flower. But through zazen, we can wake up to the fact that it's all a fantasy. Our dualistic beliefs, all of our karmic conditions arise from deluded, upside-down thinking of separation.

Ryodo Roshi, who's now president of the White Plum Asanga,[1] has a student who's from Nepal. And he told Ryodo that *dukkha* is an everyday word in his native language. It's the word we know of as the First Noble Truth of Buddhism. And we usually translate it as "suffering." But apparently, in Nepal, mothers might say to their teenagers, "You give me *dukkah*." But the translation he gives for *dukkah* is, "not going my way." I just love that. My recollection is that the word itself is derived from older words that describe a damaged wheel on your cart that clunks along as you push it. It makes me think of when you pick a grocery cart, and one wheel doesn't work.

That's *dukkah*—when things don't go our way. And that's so much more prevalent when we're attached to things, or people, or ideas. So, non-attachment is at the core of the Buddha Way. How do I get attached to my job, to a relationship, to this glorious spring day, to this beautiful flower? And of course, one of the most dangerous ones is the attachment to enlightenment. But what is enlightenment? It's just the flower. Not my ideas of it, not what I gain or learn from it. Just sniff!

I recently had a tough moment—a friend of mine died by suicide. Every time we'd have a dance party, I would dance with her to our favorite dance song, "I wanna dance with somebody . . . with somebody who loves me." It sounds like a greedy song, a thirsty song. But the reason I love it so much is that it brings people together with immense joy and appreciation for each

DREAMY PEONIES

other. She and I would just connect so deeply, dancing to that song. She really embodied that selfless joy of connection. But she had lost two babies. And the grief for her was so overwhelming. She *knew* that she should pick herself up and just go on with her life, and she did everything she could to push through. But in the end, the pain just overwhelmed her—that grief of things really not going her way. I don't pass judgment on her at all. Her karma was hers to navigate. But it exemplifies how deeply we can suffer when we attach to this dream of our life, and the dream of how we think it should be.

Initially, I told you there are two ways to look at this koan. One is—don't be attached. Be with things as they are. That's the end of suffering or *dukkha*. And the other, slightly more subtle aspect of this koan is about seeing everything, absolutely everything, as empty. The whole damn thing is just a dream, constantly changing. There's never anything to attach to in the first place. Bernie talked about this as the first of the Three Tenets of the Zen Peacemakers, which is "Not-Knowing." No separation means to see all of life as Not-Knowing, a wispy dream. And when we really see our universe as a dreamy manifestation of Not-Knowing, what arises from us is wisdom and compassion.

Even in the midst of wanting what we can't have, or hating what we do have, because it's all happening in a dream, it's perfect, as it is. So, on one hand—don't be attached. Allow life to be as it is. And on the other hand—even our delusions and attachments are empty and perfect as they are. Our practice is to cultivate these two understandings as one.

FULL CIRCLE

Recently somebody said that once you're 80, you can just do whatever you want. And my dear Dharma brother Shishin Roshi said, "Boy, I wish I could, but my vows always get in the way." That reminds me of this dance between the innate freedom of our true self, which is free from circumstances, and our vows to be of service and make circumstances better. So, we continue to always practice the Precepts, to work on our greed, anger, and ignorance through practice. Wake up to what that peony really is. And then put it in a basket for others.

MANIFESTING THE THREE TREASURES

Sometimes we forget to talk about the basic stuff. I will be facilitating a workshop next Saturday on Council practice and communication. This talk is an introduction to that workshop. I was struck by what Erick Jeong Gak Wilkins said last week: "the most important thing is connecting with each other." That's the Sangha Treasure—connecting with each other and being able to show up for others. That's how I see Council practice, being there for each other. And that's also how I see the form of governance that we use here at Sweetwater Zen Center—the circle form—working together collectively to make decisions and create programs etc., instead of relying on hierarchy and vertical power dynamics. And often, it takes way more time getting things done working as a circle, letting everybody say what they have to say, working through the places where we disagree. It's a struggle to work that way, dedicated to consensual decision making. In some ways, we'd prefer to have someone who we really trust just tell us what to do.

So, I wanted to talk about the Sangha Treasure, but with a little overview of the Three Treasures more generally. I think all Buddhist sects use the Three Treasures as a teaching. I could be wrong, but most do. They're very fundamental to the teachings of the Buddha. And I often refer back to a talk by Bernie Glassman Roshi, my teacher, on the Three Treasures. He starts off by talking about the phrase *namo*, which we actually chant in the service we did today—*The Gate of Sweet Nectar*. *Namo* is an old Sanskrit word that means, "be one with".

Sometimes we say "take refuge" in the Three Treasures. But that kind of implies, "Let them take care of me in some kind of magical way." But what *namo* means is to be it. So, I don't translate *namo* as "take refuge." Let's say, "be it", which is what the ancients said. Later in the *Gate of Sweet Nectar* service, we chant about being one with each of the Five Buddha Families; the connection, the emptiness, the wisdom, the action and the abundance. These five aspects of the awakened being comprise a Buddhist mandala. And at the center of this mandala is the Buddha Family of Emptiness. The Three Treasures—Buddha, Dharma, and Sangha—come out of that emptiness, or what Bernie ultimately preferred to call not-knowing.

In our tradition, we have many different ways of talking about what the Buddha, Dharma, and Sangha Treasures are. Though, when you look up writings and articles, many may offer one, basic way of looking at them. I wanted to give you a little more nuanced view,

MANIFESTING THE THREE TREASURES

especially looking at the Sangha treasure, in the context of Council practice, circle work and generally connecting with each other.

The Buddha Treasure can be seen as waking up from a swoon, like Victorian ladies did when they fell in love. That kind of falling in love where you just get taken up by something—some form of greed, anger or ignorance. You get totally taken up by falling in love, by lust, or neediness or even hatred. When you wake up from that swoon, that's one way to see the Buddha Treasure.[2] It's an undefinable experience of awakening. And that's what the koans are about. That's what all the books are about. What is that waking up? What did Buddha find out? What is Buddha in terms of the actual person who woke up 2500 years ago? And of course, the person we know as Shakyamuni Buddha, that historic figure is not the *first* Buddha. During the Fusatsu ceremony, we chant *namo* a lot, as we embody all Buddhas and Bodhisattvas, starting with the "Past Seven Buddhas." (Fusatsu is an atonement ceremony that consists of atoning, renewing vows to practice the Precepts, and invoking the names of the Buddhas and Bodhisattvas, revealing that they are no other than myself). When you take Jukai and make a lineage chart, before the Buddha, there are Seven Past Buddhas. This represents the fact that there wasn't a first person who awakened. There were Buddhas before Buddha. Of course there were! So, Shakyamuni Buddha was not the first one to figure this out. Figure what out? Simply realizing *This*. Because *This* is who we are. What Buddha realizes is the fact of our life as just *This*.

Then, as the Fusatsu ceremony continues, we are one with Maitreya Buddha, the Buddha that comes after the end of this time or *kalpa*, which is an era or epoch so long, it's as if an angel came down every thousand years and brushed its wing against the side of a huge cliff, and the time it would take for that cliff to be worn down is a *kalpa*. An unimaginably long time. So when this *kalpa* ends, then the next Buddha is Maitreya Buddha. Who is that Maitreya Buddha? *Namo* Maitreya Buddha. Who is it that, right now, chanting Fusatsu, is being one with Maitreya Buddha? That's you! You are the one that comes after the end of the *kalpa*. Be one with Maitreya Buddha.

Manjushri Bodhisattva represents wisdom. And again, wisdom arises out of emptiness. Wisdom discerns the differences that arise out of emptiness. So be wisdom. Avalokiteshvara is compassion, and in the Fusatsu ceremony, we're one with all of them, and we bring them here, we bring all of the Buddhas here. So, the Buddha Treasure can be the historical figure, or it can refer to these other Buddhas and Bodhisattvas — Samantabhadra Bodhisattva is practice, meditation. Being one with Samantabhadra is being zazen.

So, the Buddha Treasure can refer to the historical figure who woke up, the other Buddhas and Bodhisattvas, and it can also refer to that which these Buddhas awaken to itself — the emptiness, or oneness, of all things. Furthermore, a third way to see the Buddha Treasure is as the images and statues of Buddhas and Bodhisattvas. Some people, especially in the West, are uncomfortable with the iconography and the ritual of Buddhism. But they are an essential part of it. That's what we've been talking about lately, especially in studying Zenju Earthlyn Manuel Roshi. We've been looking at the concern of some of our Asian ancestors and friends, around the West's reduction of Buddhism to just mindfulness and breathing techniques. A complete view of Buddhism includes ritual, and ritual includes the images and practicing with the images. So, the Buddha Treasure is all of these things.

Then the Dharma Treasure, too, can have three meanings. One is what the Buddha said, what the Buddha taught, like this, like a Dharma talk. This is, supposedly, Dharma. And I'm doing the best I can to be Dharma—to talk about what Buddha found out. The Dharma Treasure can also refer to all the differences, or phenomena that arise out of oneness, or emptiness. The koan that Kosei is working on for *Shuso Hossen*[3] talks about how the "sutras are your very life." What are the sutras? What are the Buddha's teachings? It's your life and everything in it. And lastly, just like the Buddha Treasure can refer to the actual images and statues of Buddha, the Dharma Treasure can refer to the actual books and texts that contain the Buddha's teachings, the sutras and liturgy. So those are the three ways to see the Dharma Treasure.

And then the Sangha Treasure, which is what I'm emphasizing today. It can get controversial, how we see the Sangha. Bernie always liked to call the Sangha, "harmony". The oneness is Buddha, the manyness is Dharma, and the harmony, or fusion of the Buddha and Dharma is the first way to see the Sangha Treasure. It can also be seen as the community of people who practice together. All of us here at SWZC make up the Sangha. And the third way to see the Sangha Treasure is as the lineage of Dharma teachers from Shakyamuni Buddha all the way down to those teaching today. It is those who have direct Dharma transmission and join the lineage with Buddha. Given these three aspects of the Sangha Treasure, when I think about Sangha, it generally feels like connectedness. And I think that fits in with Bernie saying "Harmony".

A few of you might remember Werner Erhard and his teachings. One thing he really stressed was that self-realization was the first step. The main point is working together, collective realization. Many of you are practicing because you want to see what Buddha saw. That's one of the aspirations that we have. And a lot of Buddhist commentary will say, "Do you wanna see what Buddha saw? Then do zazen! And don't waste a minute!" And all of that kind of talk. And I, myself, put many years into, "I wanna see what Buddha saw. I wanna have that experience." And then, at the point of that experience, we also realize that *everything* is Buddha. All the differences, every thing, person, piece of grass, fire, global warming, everything is Buddha. Like Kosei's koan says, every little thing in my life is Buddha. And, then, the continuous practice of our life, the Sangha practice, is not just about that experience or realization that everything is Buddha. It is cultivating that realization collectively. Group enlightenment, or shared wisdom is one way to talk about it. Of course, waking up to our true nature and manifesting that awakening in every aspect of our lives is not a linear process. At the same that we practice waking up we are practicing connection with our community and serving all beings. We don't wait to serve until we reach some kind of awakening goal.

Most of us struggle with relationships on one level or another. I was reading Truman Capote. There's that new documentary out, so I went and read some of his work. Something he emphasized was that we will never know how other people think about us. How many of us really share exactly how we think about each other? And course, it's constantly changing how we think about each other. But to practice connection, there is a feeling, there's an experience when we connect. I think I feel it most when dancing, just dancing together. All of a sudden, the many selves disappear and the ideas and separation disappears. Or maybe in team sports, I've never been a team sports person, but I imagine that's a place where you can feel that. Or singing, singing together. Or doing *samu*, work practice, together.

Council is the main Sangha connection practice that we do here. It's one of the practices we do to really be there for each other. It's a practice of really being another person, to truly listen as if another's words were mine. Even though they're an idiot, and what they're saying doesn't make any sense. Even though it's boring. It really is just the same as zazen. It's boring; it's hard; it hurts; it's uncomfortable. We have all sorts of things coming up just being with each other. And then there are moments—those of you who've done a lot of Council practice know—there's moments in Council when we are one, and we're together as one body sharing this moment.

FULL CIRCLE

So, that's what I want to talk about during the Communication Workshop, some training in Council practice, which has to do with listening, wholly. Not like "holy, holy, holy", but wholly, being one with not knowing each other, and learning to express ourselves authentically, to speak from the heart, which means not to spin, not to talk so people like us, not to talk so we seem smart, but to really be authentic to our experience. That's what we're going to keep working on. And that's all I have to say.

CIRCLE STRUCTURE AS THE THREE TREASURES

The Sweetwater Zen Center (SWZC) Board recently approved the *Sangha Sutra*, which is a document that covers all the aspects of practicing in a healthy community. One of these aspects is how shared leadership and the Circle Structure work at SWZC. We didn't invent the Circle Structure, but we've spent a long time adapting it for our sangha in particular.

Circles themselves are a major part of Buddhist teachings. Even our lineage of Zen masters is presented as a circular chart in certain cases. The lineage starts with the Past Seven Buddhas, then Shakyamuni Buddha transmitted to Mahakashyapa, who transmitted to Ananda, and so on, until it got to me. And because pretty much only men have been able to practice and inherit the Dharma until recently, I have the distinction of being the first female name on our lineage chart. Scholars now say that some of those lineage holders, like Prajnatara, could have possibly been women. But traditionally they are all seen as men. And even though we list them chronologically, to see everything as one means that each one of us is the Past Seven Buddhas, is Prajnatara. If you do take *Jukai*, and make an official statement of your intention to practice, you have to make your own lineage chart, or *kechimyaku*. And you'll see that after my name, there's a red line that goes back to the past seven Buddhas. So, the lineage is actually presented as a circle in the *kechimyaku*.

We also see a circle with the Japanese *enso* image. Circles show up in a lot of koans, too. There's one where a monk asks about Buddha, and another monk draws a circle in the air. Then there's a bunch of chatter about that circle. But basically, that circle represents oneness, our true nature. It represents equality, no higher or lower. So, implementing circles in our power structures is a very powerful tool for overcoming the patriarchal, top-down models of power that we have been conditioned in for so long. We're so accustomed to a boss, someone at the top. And I'm not sure that sticking to that paradigm is how we evolve, grow, and heal. It makes more sense to me that we share power and leadership.

Top-down power isn't just potentially oppressive and toxic for those at the bottom. It's tough on the leader. There's a lot of stress for a boss who has all the power and responsibility. That position can lend itself to burnout, corruption and resentment. And that's not good for leading. So, a circular power structure both empowers the members of a community, and honors the wellbeing of those who do take on more responsibility.

It's not that we're aiming for a completely egalitarian

CIRCLE STRUCTURE AS THE THREE TREASURES

culture, where everyone is totally equal in responsibility. In order for Zen training to have integrity, there are teachers and students, trainers and trainees, a Board of Directors with a president and secretary etc. There are positions of certain power and responsibility, *and* at the same time, we work within Circles, or committees, where those with more responsibility use that position to empower others. So, it gets a little tricky—trying to horizontalize power and cultivate collective leadership, while simultaneously honoring the vertical power dynamics of traditional Zen training. We will make missteps and have to massage things as we learn more. But it's a great step in the direction of dismantling patriarchal norms that have caused so much harm in so many communities over time.

The specific Circle Structure we've developed here at SWZC is based around the Three Treasures—Buddha, Dharma and Sangha. And I always go back to one of Bernie Roshi's talks on the Three Treasures when I'm thinking of ways to talk about them. It's a talk he gave in 1977, right after his Dharma Transmission from Maezumi Roshi. I was there, I remember hearing this talk. One of the main points of his talk is that our practice is to "be" the Three Treasures. Very often, Buddhist literature talks about "taking refuge" in the Three Treasures. For example, in the *Gate of Sweet Nectar* service we do every Sunday, we chant, "Buddham Saranam Gachami, Dhammam Saranam Gachami, Sangham Saranam Gachami," which means, "I take refuge in" Buddha, Dharma and Sangha. But Bernie's point is that to truly honor the Three Treasures, we must see ourselves *as* them. And in a way, "taking refuge" and "being" aren't really that different. When we truly embody what we naturally are—the Buddha, the Dharma and the Sangha—we find safety, we find our true home. That is where we can truly find refuge.

This has nothing to do with the word Buddha. For you, the first treasure could be Christ, it could be Yahweh, Oneness, Spirit, whatever word you use to describe our inherent unity with everything in the universe. That's what we mean by "Buddha." There is just this one body, right now! Sometimes we call this the *Dharmakaya*—the world as emptiness, complete oneness—which is nothing other than our life. Buddha is the morning dew, it is our disappointment, our achievement, all the joy and suffering of the world. And the nature of Buddha is empty, without self. We make up identities and definitions through years and lifetimes of karmic activity. The treasure of Buddha is the fact that self, identity and definition are all empty, all delusion. And so really, that's all you need to say.

However, if we take that all the way, seeing everything as empty must be empty too. So, we can't stop there. We can't stop anywhere. And that's why we have Three Treasures and endless teachings. The second treasure is Dharma, which can be seen as: all phenomena, all the differences that arise out of the empty oneness. Being the Dharma Treasure is how we cultivate wisdom and discernment, in service to all beings. It acknowledges suffering and joy, which cease to exist when we become the Buddha Treasure. We identify and define things so that we can take care of ourselves and others.

CIRCLE STRUCTURE AS THE THREE TREASURES

When you're 75, you get to sit around and not remember anybody's name. When you're young, you get to work really hard and build things, remember everything. These differences are the Dharma Treasure.

And then the third treasure is Sangha—the unity of the first two treasures. It's the perfect harmony of Buddha and Dharma, of emptiness and phenomena, of oneness and diversity. The Sangha Treasure can be seen in the teachings in our morning service. The *Heart Sutra* says "form is emptiness, emptiness is form." We also chant the *San Do Kai*, or, *Identity of Relative and Absolute*. Maezumi Roshi always said that the term "Identity" in this context means the total inter-penetration of Relative (Dharma) and Absolute (Buddha). The differences are oneness. The oneness is all the differences. Simple! So, these sutras are essentially an expression of the Sangha Treasure.

We decided to use the Three Treasures as a model around which to construct our Circle Structure at SWZC. The Buddha Circles are responsible for all the aspects of training. That includes the Leadership Circle, the Teachers Circle, the Events Circle, the Jikido Circle, the Chiden Circle, the Ino Circle etc. These circles represent the teachings of no-self, oneness. They manage programming, the zazen schedule, altars, teachings, services and ceremonies. Then, the Dharma Circles are in charge of the administration, and represent the wisdom and discernment of the Zen Center. These circles include the Board of Directors, the Buildings and Grounds Circle, the Residency Circle, the Fundraising Circle, the Membership Circle etc. And, of course, there are arguments for saying that the Dharma Circles belong on the Buddha side, and the Buddha Circles belong on the Dharma side, because the fact is that they are totally inter-penetrated.

Which brings us to the Sangha Circle. Just like with the Three Treasures, the Sangha Circle manifests as the total oneness of Buddha and Dharma. So, the living embodiment of the Circles that we take on as a community is itself the Sangha Circle. Engagement in the Circle Structure is itself the Sangha Treasure in action.

We have two Circles that are kind of inactive until necessary—The H.E.A.R. Circle and the Elders Circle. The Hearing, Ethics and Reconciliation Circle (H.E.A.R.) acts kind of like a grievance council. If you have a conflict or need to report misconduct at the Zen Center, and it doesn't feel safe to talk directly to the people involved in the incident, the H.E.A.R. circle can act as a sounding board, a mediating body, or in extreme circumstances, the H.E.A.R. will adjudicate an official grievance filing.

The Elders Circle is a body of trusted, veteran Zen teachers in our lineage that can be consulted if there's a disagreement between the Board and the Abbot. If the Board says, "Ya know, if we had a bar during sesshin, we'd probably make a lot of money," and the Abbot says, "No, no bar," and they can't reach an agreement, then the Elders Circle is convened to help find a resolution. If the Abbot has abused their power in a way that's harmful to the sangha and it can't be resolved by the Board and the H.E.A.R Circle, that would be a time for

CIRCLE STRUCTURE AS THE THREE TREASURES

the Elder Circle to be called, to decide how to address the accusations about the Abbot.

So, hopefully you can start to see how the Circle Structure is constructed to spread power throughout the sangha, so that there are thorough checks and balances on everyone, and so that everyone in the sangha feels empowered. The whole idea behind the Circles is to open up communication and access to everyone in the community, so that we talk to each other, communicate our wisdom, and hold each other accountable, so we can avoid power abuse and resentment in our community. And I believe that the more we engage in these models of shared leadership, the more clearly we can see the emptiness of our differences, the diversity that comes out of our oneness, and the harmony we can create in the world.

THE SANGHA SUTRA

We've been working for a long time on our grievance procedure at Sweetwater Zen Center. Until recently, our grievance procedure has basically just been based around the Precepts, without any formal process. And of course, the thing about the Precepts is that they're not cut and dry rules to follow. And that's one major aspect of Zen practice and enlightenment—not getting rigid or stuck on any idea or rule. And while that's an incredible practice, being in harmony with impermanence, when it comes to ethics and justice in community, having clear policies and practices can be very helpful for preventing or alleviating harm. Even not being rigid is something we can't be rigid about.

I remember there was a little boy who was part of the community at Yokoji Zen Mountain Center, where I was co-abbot, many years ago. And for those of you who haven't been there, the Seventh Day Adventist camp is very close to Yokoji. So, this boy started hanging out with the Seventh Day Adventists, and one day, he announced to all of us that he was going to be a Seventh

Day Adventist. Part of the reason was probably the horses and swimming pool they had there. But another aspect of his attraction to them was probably their strict clarity around rules. And, especially for a little boy, clarity and directness can be very attractive and offer stability. That's what's so beautiful and, at the same time, difficult to stick with in Zen practice—trying to embody impermanence and Not-Knowing.

Even the Buddhist Precepts are studied from multiple angles and perspectives, some of which may completely contradict each other. We talk about this every other month when we do the *Day of Reflection,* which entails doing the Fusatsu ceremony—renewal of vows to practice the Precepts—and we have council around one Precept in particular. Fusatsu is an ancient ceremony. Even back in Buddha's time, the sangha did Fusatsu together, maybe even twice a month. And they did their version of council too. Sometimes we think council is some brand new Western invention. But in Buddha's time, they came together as a sangha, and everyone shared about their practice within the community, and how they may have caused harm to themselves or others. Accountability and atonement have always been central to the Buddha Way.

Some people get lost in the sitting, *samadhi* part of Zen. But ethics and atonement are a major aspect of our practice. So, for a sangha to develop strong core values, and clear pathways to accountability and healing is incredibly important. In the old days, when I was practicing with Maezumi Roshi at ZCLA, we were pretty loosey goosey about ethics, and it really caused a lot of harm. But out of those mistakes, teachers in our lineage—the White Plum Asanga—have been working together for decades to craft what's called the *Sangha Sutra*, a comprehensive document outlining all the aspects of an ethical community that takes accountability for preventing and repairing misconduct and harm. ZCLA has already adopted theirs, and we are close to having a final version for us here at SWZC. And I'm so thankful to Roshi Egyoku and the ZCLA sangha for putting so much work into their *Sangha Sutra,* and allowing us to pretty much use theirs, with our own adaptations to fit our sangha.

For me, a very important part of our *Sangha Sutra* is the detailing of our efforts towards a more horizontal power structure for the Zen center. Namely, that's the Circle Structure, which I encountered in my work with my teacher Roshi Bernie, and Lama Tsultrim Allione. So it's been part of my vision here at SWZC to shift from the vertical power hierarchies we see in traditional Zen temples, to a more horizontal one, where leadership is shared and collective decision making is prioritized. That's not to say that we don't have positions and empowerments and staff members and senior students. We don't do away completely with power structure. So, the *Sangha Sutra*, gives a full lay out of how these power dynamics play out in our sangha. It also outlines our code of ethics, and it offers a very clear and in-depth grievance procedure that anyone and everyone can participate in.

What exactly is *sangha*? We talk about it in different ways. One way to see *sangha* is a community of people who practice together. So the original Buddhist *sangha* would have been the disciples of the Buddha. They were monks and nuns, people who had taken the vow of celibacy, who had left their home and family. They were all totally committed to waking up to what the Buddha woke up to. There's a very strong, intimate sense of *sangha* in that kind collective commitment. Today, we often use *sangha* more broadly, to refer to a larger community of people that support or are associated with a practice center. There are many people in our *sangha* who aren't Buddhists at all. Their primary practice is Judaism, Christianity, or yoga, but being a part of SWZC helps support them in that practice. Which is great!

Our *Sangha Sutra* is pretty comprehensive; it's over 60 pages long. But I wanted to share with you a little bit of the introduction. And again, most of this was written by Egyoku Roshi and her sangha, and we're so grateful for the work they put into it.

WHAT IS THE SANGHA SUTRA?

A sangha is formed when three or more people practice the awakened way together and embrace the spirit of the Three Treasures of Buddha, Dharma and Sangha. The Buddha is awakened realization, the Dharma, the teachings of awakening, and the Sangha, the community of practitioners. Sweetwater Zen Center's mission and vision strive to embody collective awakening. This means that practice at

THE SANGHA SUTRA

Sweetwater Zen Center is designed as a skillful means for awakening together as a sangha.

. . . the word "sutra" translates as thread. And each individual is a thread of the sangha fabric. Fabric is typically made of the warp—the threads that run lengthwise—and the woof—the threads that weave around the warp running crosswise. For the sangha fabric, the warp is made of practice and the Three Treasures. And the woof is how each member engages with them. What kind of fabric are we weaving together? What patterns are being revealed?

Together, we weave the fabric of the sangha treasure by illuminating the Dharma of emptiness, interconnection, and impermanence. Aligning ourselves with these pillars of reality fosters living in harmony, as we are called forth to see others as ourselves and ourselves as others. With this fundamental view, we honor diversity and become skilled in addressing conflicts as a path to deeper interconnectedness. All fabric inevitably wears out. Holes and tears appear, and seams rip apart. But fabric is strengthened in its mending. And so we approach conflict within the sangha as an opportunity for growth.

The Sangha Sutra is not a rigid set of rules. Rather, it provides guidance on how to live harmoniously together, in accord with the ever-changing circumstances of life. Life is nuanced, complex, and full of paradoxes. Although there are no fixed answers, there are practices that help us become flexible and

> *responsive with wisdom and compassion. Rooted in the fundamental principle of doing no harm, this Sangha Sutra challenges us to go beyond our self-centered views, to develop a broader, more selfless perspective on what is needed in any given situation.*

I also wanted to share some of the part that talks about the White Plum's history, which many of you know well.

> *This Sangha Sutra is partially inspired by mistakes made by our past teachers and ancestors, and the need for healing after the damage left in their wake. Questions came up about the nature of enlightenment, the human flaws of Zen teachers, and the psychological foundation for practice. At that time, American Zen centers lacked the structure for dealing with ethical misconduct and accountability. And the intersection of Asian and American culture led to further misunderstandings about Zen culture and ethics.*
>
> *It was still acknowledged that spiritual wisdom does not necessarily include psychological, emotional maturity, nor that our own ideas of power, sex, and race are not exempt from scrutiny. This led to dysfunctional sangha cultures that practitioners spiritually bypass, leaving little room for insight and accountability. With a concentrated emphasis on zazen alone, the effects of conditioning and cause and effect were investigated in these early days.*

THE SANGHA SUTRA

Times of crisis can be followed by years of sincere self-reflection and discernment. This practice can inform us when we are not in alignment, not in harmony. In the very act of living, our wheels naturally go out of alignment, our fabric frays. Regardless of the reasons, we admit our errors, atone and commit to doing better. Just as we say about Precepts: we drink from the glass, so the glass gets dirty, we clean the glass, and we drink from it. Realignment is not a one-time action; it is continual. The Sangha Sutra is about caring for the fabric we are weaving together, and mending its tears again and again.

This weaving that we do together as a community is bound to fall apart. But that's where we have the opportunity to mend, forgive, and heal. And that's how we grow even stronger together. It reminds me of that beautiful lyric from that Tool song, "I know the pieces fit, cuz I watched them fall away." When our communities and relationships fall apart, can we show up to knit that back together? The practices we do here—zazen, council, ritual and ceremony—are powerful mending tools.

The sangha has been working on finessing the *Sangha Sutra* for almost 20 years. And I know that at times it's been a frustrating process. But finding real clarity on a lot of these issues takes time. And I know that the fabric of our sangha will be stronger as we become more familiar with the content of the document, and integrate it into our practice as a community.

THE BATH PATH I

Today's a very auspicious day. It's Father's Day. And also, today is Juneteenth, our new federal holiday. That's something to celebrate—the end of slavery. Well, of course it wasn't the end of slavery; there's still slavery today. But it marked the end of legal slavery in America. What a horrendous thing. I'm so happy that Juneteenth is now recognized as an official holiday. And thanks to all the fathers.

Today I want to talk about this koan, which is a very unique koan. It comes from the *Surangama Sutra*, which is ancient. And the event found in this koan happened in India. This is an old, old story. Many of our koans are old stories, but most are stories from China, many years after Buddhism spread from India to China. But this koan's in India and is part of this section of the *Surangama Sutra*:

> In ancient times, there were 16 Bodhisattvas who, at the monk's bath time, following the rule, filed into the bath. Suddenly they experienced realization

through the touch of the water. You Zen worthies, how will you understand their saying: "Experiencing the subtle and clear touch, we have achieved the status of sons of Buddha." You'll only be able to attain this after seven times piercing and eight times breaking through.

This story from the *Surangama Sutra* is also presented in the *Blue Cliff Record*. When I was practicing at a monastery in Japan, we had bath time every day, which is unusual. It is usually once a week, but we got to do it every day. In the monastery there's a big bathhouse. You shower first, and then you go and soak in the hot tub. It was so cold there, and there were no heaters or anything. So that was the one time your body could really warm up. I was there with Roshi Enkyo, and she and I were the only women. So we got to go into the assistant abbot's private bath *before* he did. But anyway, this is something that's gone on for a long time—the ritual of bathing together, doing hot tub together. It's certainly a very Japanese thing to do, and it's part of the Zen training program.

Reading the commentary for this koan, it says that since this happened in India, there's a good chance that the bath was cold. Because it's so hot in India, the relief would be going into a *cold* bath. But anyway, 16 people went into the bath and were simultaneously enlightened. The reason I think this koan is so important is because I believe it's one of the few koans about *mutual* enlightenment. Usually, koans present a teacher and a student, and the teacher offers a turning word or does something skillful, and the student awakens. Or there's the sound of a pebble and somebody gets enlightened. This is the only one I can think of right now where the group gets enlightened at the same time. And I think that's so important for this age of Zen around the whole world. We're really emphasizing the importance of the Sangha Treasure and the importance of non-distinction. We practice working together as circles, or committees, deemphasizing traditional, hierarchical power structures. Or at least we try to combine vertical and horizontal power structures.

Some Buddhist hierarchical structures exalt the Abbot of the temple as super enlightened, and there are maybe some other teachers that are super enlightened. Then there are senior students who are a little bit enlightened. And then there are the newer practitioners who seemingly have no realization. That's a traditional hierarchical structure found in many Zen practice centers. Within this context, you're expected to do whatever the ones "above" you tell you to do. That's a vertical power structure. The horizontal recognizes the fact that, as we are, each of us is enlightened. And I think that's true. If you show up at a Zen center, you probably have some kind of sense of the oneness of all things. Nowadays, there's so much spirituality—yoga and tai chi, etc.—and many traditions teaching the oneness of all things. So, people often come to the Zen center with a sense of that. I think it's important to emphasize that—each of us brings our own understanding into a community, into the sangha. And each of us also brings the places where we're holding on, our resistance.

FULL CIRCLE

One thing that the commentary to this story says is that fundamentally, there are two kinds of mind. There's the ordinary mind, which we operate in on a day-to-day basis. That mind gets caught endlessly in the illusion of life and death, the *skandhas*,[4] and attachment. That's what we sometimes call our deluded mind, or our karmic mind. And it says that pure perception is *not* delusion. Sometimes we hear that feelings are delusions; anger and desire are delusions. But before we add our ideas on top, feeling emotions is just pure perception. The delusion is what we do with it. So, when we feel angry, if we harm somebody in reaction, that's the delusion of holding onto that anger. When we have desire, if we go take something from someone else, if we go and steal something, same thing. Just the perception of these feelings is "pure." (I'm using these dualistic words, so you have to forgive me). And we get into trouble when we add on our own thoughts, evaluations and concepts to that perception.

So, in terms of the two kinds of minds, the first is this ordinary mind that "goes down the rabbit hole" as I call it. Something happens and I feel jealous, then I go down the rabbit hole of how terrible that person is, or how terrible I am, or how I have to do something different, or life sucks, or whatever. That's this entangled mind.

The second mind is the everlasting true mind, which is our real nature, the state of Buddha. So, when these monks in the koan—it says men, but they could easily have been all sorts of different genders—when these people experience the sensation of water at that moment, they are all awakened. And what does that awakening mean? It can be different for each person, but it's essentially seeing a little bit into the fact that this entangled mind, as it is, is perfect. Oh wow! "This is just anger," or, "This is just greed." And then I don't have to get more deeply entangled in it. I don't have to create and follow a story. I don't have to act reactively and get in trouble. So, just for a moment, these folks in the tub realize that together.

That's the point that I think is so important, and so relevant for us is in community: all of us have some insight. All of us have some amazing insight into the oneness of all things, and into the wonderful, joyous, pure true self. And, all of us get entangled very easily. Just break a glass, and all of a sudden I'm like, "I never do anything right. I've always been so clumsy."

Then the question is, how can we support each other as a community in getting out of that rabbit hole when we fall into it? How do we collectively shift our minds to seeing the oneness, together?

Now we've officially passed our Sangha Sutra—a comprehensive document that outlines all the aspects of a healthy community, with healthy boundaries and shared leadership structures. I highly recommend reading through it, it is on SWZC's website. The Sangha Sutra has tons of advice and techniques for getting out of the rabbit hole, how to communicate, how to work with trauma and so much more. And like the commentary says, that "ordinary mind" is so entangled, and our childhood trauma and all of our karmic stuff make up the tangles.

The point isn't to support each other so that this or that person becomes some great enlightened being. We do it together to support our mutual, collective awakening. That's why I love this koan.

A long time ago, I did some of Werner Erhard's EST training, and I enjoyed it. There were some things that were problematic, but it was very helpful to me. One thing that Werner Erhard really emphasized is that initially, there's my own insight into the oneness of all things, and the meaninglessness of all the extra stuff I put on top of just this. But then, the community must work on waking up collectively, expanding so much that eventually the whole world works together on waking up. So, he also really emphasized collective awakening as essential to spiritual practice. If you just do it for yourself, that's okay, but what about doing it with all beings?

Reading more from this commentary on the koan, he says that the reason we fall into delusion is because we believe in life and death, and the concept of time itself. This mind is dependent on perceived objects—getting the perfect partner, getting the degree, getting the car, feeling or being some kind of way. We get entangled, believing that our true nature is one of greed, desire, and anger.

If we look at the *Surangama Sutra* itself, it apparently talks about three main themes. The first is awakening. Just like in the Zen Peacemaker Three Tenets, the first is not-knowing—pure, empty, no life, no death, no good, no bad. It's the oneness of all things, the Buddha mind. And zazen is the best way I know of to really become intimate with this.

The second theme from the sutra is our complex mind, with all its differentiation, emotions, desires, belief in life and death. It is our karmic situation. This is like the second of the Three Tenets—bearing witness to the joys and pains of the differentiated universe, and our complex minds that perceive it. And apparently, the *Surangama Sutra* talks about how to deal with this complex mind. It's similar to how our Sangha Sutra talks about addressing our complex minds. It goes through things like the importance of therapy and mindfulness and many, many different ways to work on our karmic conditions, which Zen practice doesn't necessarily offer directly.

The third theme is an emphasis on the Precepts. This still mirrors the Three Tenets, the third of which is loving action, which is essentially what the Precepts are. They aren't some burdensome chores that we have to do, so we go to heaven or whatever. The Precepts are the natural functioning of the Bodhisattva. It's very interesting to me how this commentary defines Buddha and Bodhisattva. It could be the first time I've heard it this way and I kind of like it. It says that a Bodhisattva is anyone who has awakened to their true nature, but is still willfully attached to the concept of serving others. And it says that a Buddha—which is very, very rare according to this writer; personally, I don't know about that—doesn't set out to help others. A Buddha serves without the notion of serving. They serve others as naturally as breathing.

So, it's not that Buddha just realizes it's all one and, thus, just simply doesn't care. It's that Buddha doesn't even conceive of the differences between me and you, us and them. For a Buddha, to help others is helping yourself, period. There isn't the thought, "oh, I should pick up that trash." There is just picking up the trash. So that's pretty much what I wanted to present today. The main thing is that as a sangha, we can awaken together. And I think that's a great vow for our practice community—to wake up together, and to help each other with the struggles that we face. We all have struggles. So how do we help each other in the places where we get stuck, the places that create suffering for us? Take a dip and find out!

THIS, THAT & NEITHER

Today, I want to look at Case Three of the *Blue Cliff Record*—"Great Master Ba Is Unwell."

> *The superintendent of the temple asked Master Ba,*
> *"How is your health these days?"*
> *The great master said, "Sun-faced Buddha,*
> *moon-faced Buddha."*

I initially chose this because the Zen Center has had a run in with COVID. And it made me think about sickness and how we work with it. It's also the beginning of *Rohatsu* week, which is the week of Buddha's Awakening. Traditionally, in a monastery, everyone sits for eight days, from December first to the eighth, which is Bodhi Day.

There is such a thing as an awakening experience. It is a real thing, and it's the core of the Buddha Way. Many might argue with me, but I'll say it's the essential spirit of *Rohatsu*. And while the experience is indeed real, its nature is totally ungraspable. So, talking about it is very difficult. But I can say that on the Zen path, zazen is essential for the awakening experience. Siddhartha, before becoming the historical Buddha, tried Hindu practices and ascetic practices, starving himself etc. And, after exhausting all of those methods, he just said, "I give up. I'm just going to sit here under this tree until I experience spiritual satisfaction." He had faith that there was something to awaken to, but he hadn't had the experience. So he sat, for weeks. And then one morning, he looked at the morning star and woke up. He had that experience.

And that is not some special thing that only happened to the Buddha. What he said when he woke up was, "Wonder of wonders, all beings have the wisdom and compassion of the Buddha." All beings, intrinsically, are awake. But because of delusional thinking, we don't see it. I believe that I'm separate from everybody else, that I exist, that my little bundle of greed, anger, and ignorance is a real thing. So, what we wake up to is our true nature of no-self. That is complete freedom.

I think about the *Green Flash* here in Mexico, living by the ocean. It's such a big deal. Well, I see the *Green Flash* all the time. When there are no clouds, as the sun sets over the horizon, you can see a little green flash. Usually, it's no big deal at all. It's just a little green around the sun. And so many people say they've never seen the *Green Flash*, because they think it's like the whole world turns green or something spectacular. This is like the enlightenment experience, which is different for everyone. Depending on our karma and what our practice is, we experience the flash uniquely. It's not really useful to try to judge others' experiences. We just simply catch the flash as it comes to us.

But I want you to know that it is a thing, a real experience. It's not an idea or a theory. And the way there is not like baking a cake. You can't just follow directions and get a cake. Your way is totally unique to you. Zazen is just one, very powerful tool for having that experience. It's how we quiet down our ideas and concepts, which get in the way of our having it.

At some point, when we sit for a long time—like during *Rohatsu* sesshin—we're in leg and back pain, we get caught up in worry and hatred, comparing and judging. So much bubbles up while we're sitting. All that kind of stuff famously came up for the Buddha too, as he sat under the Bodhi Tree. He envisioned beautiful women tempting him. His father came to him in a vision and said, "You have to come home and save the country." All of these distractions and attachments come up, but we stay present and aware. We don't follow them. We stay sitting, in the moment. No matter what comes up, we stay sitting. And at some point, a shift happens. No matter who you are, if you practice sincerely, it's as easy to miss as it is the floor when you take a step.

Many people study koans intellectually or philosophically, and that can be quite interesting. But sitting deeply with koans is a powerful tool on the path to this awakening experience. In that quiet place of zazen, penetrating the heart of a koan can be a shift towards awakening. And this koan about Master Ba offers a perfect example.

Let me read a bit of the introduction.

FULL CIRCLE

One device, one state, one word, one phrase.

Where's the place to let go of our little self? This very moment is without self, and is the perfect place to enter.

But even to say this is gouging a wound in healthy flesh.

To talk about the process of awakening, like I've been doing here, that's something extra. It wounds the flesh and bone of our practice. Let's just be here, without attaching concepts and labels to anything. Talking about it, it can become a nest or a den. So, if we're practicing with ideas, if we have an idea of what enlightenment is—it's love, it's everybody, it's being of service—whatever idea we have about enlightenment becomes a little nest for us, a little safe place to hold onto. In fact, awakening is becoming completely open to everything, holding on to nothing. And that's ultimate safety. That's the safety of being free from conditions and preferences. However, these awakening experiences, like the *Green Flash*, might be simple and momentary. We have this striking moment of openness and oneness, and then we start thinking about this or that, and we're right back in our nests. So, we must keep practicing. That's why practice is forever.

When the great function manifests, it does not keep to rules.

THIS, THAT & NEITHER

The Precepts help guide us. But, if we're completely one with this moment, then the next step is obvious. No need for rules to hold on to.

The aim for the moment is knowledge of the existence of the transcendent, which covers heaven and earth, but cannot be grasped.

Talk about gouging healthy flesh—"the existence of the transcendent." But he can't help it because the minute you say anything about it, it's lost. Which is, ironically, what he's trying to say.

I'm just blathering on about what enlightenment is. Please don't hang on to anything I say. Experience it for yourself. And the best way I know how to do that is with lots and lots of zazen. You really need to settle. You really need to empty the mind in order to really be: thus will do, and not thus will do too. Often, you'll hear Zen teachers say things like, "It's this, and it's that. And, it's not this, nor that." That may sound like a super wise thing to say. But it, too, is just an idea. All of it makes no sense. And it has nothing to do with waking up. Just wake up to this moment. Just be every moment and everything that's going on. Simple!

If you recall, the reason Buddha started practicing was his deep, aching question—why is there suffering? And particularly, why is there old age, sickness and death? Master Ba in this koan is on his deathbed. He is old, he's sick, and he's getting ready to die. The superintendent of the temple, who's a student of Master Ba, is of course very upset. He's grieving, he's worried, he's afraid, he's facing his own mortality too. So, when he says, "How is your health these days?" it's a deep existential question. Why is there suffering? What about me? What is death? There's grieving, there's sadness in his question. We see his despair, which any of us feel when someone we love passes. And the great master says, "Sun-faced Buddha, moon-faced Buddha." Absolutely everything is Buddha. That's his realization in a few beautiful words. And again, words can't truly convey it, but it's one memorable way to express it verbally.

Sometimes, it's the sun; sometimes, it's the moon. This time of the year must be auspicious—the Buddha got enlightened, and Christ was born—when the darkness is longer than the lightness. Some of us think that darkness is worse than lightness. We talk about the shadow or the darkness as a bad thing. The brightness is a good thing. But when we wake up, we see they're just two aspects of Buddha. Just like life and death, sickness and health are too.

Oh, I love what we wrote in the fundraising letter this year. It says something like, "Sweetwater Zen Center exists to help wake up the true, authentic self." It's not like I have to wake it up. It wakes up naturally because I give it a little space, just a teeny, tiny bit of space from my yada, yada, yada. Calm that down. Just shut up. And allow the authentic self to wake up. And the Zen Center is a place to do that—lots of zazen. A little bit of meditation is pretty cool, but a week of meditation . . . that's how we come face-to-face with all the ways we're stuck, hanging on to this body and mind.

THIS, THAT & NEITHER

I want you to know deeply your true self of both this and that, and not this nor that. But please don't make it an intellectual exercise. Just allow the sun to wake up; allow the moon to wake up. All ideas are false, including this one.

TWO ENDS TO SUFFERING

The Four Noble Truths: life is suffering, there's a cause of suffering, there's an end to suffering, and the Eightfold Path. It's very hard to get this. I was enjoying listening to the *Gate of Sweet Nectar* service this morning, because the *Gate of Sweet Nectar* directly addresses the end of suffering. "Being one with the Unconditioned Tathagata." Be one with the unconditioned—just this. And I also love that the *Gate of Sweet Nectar* tells you exactly what to do. I was amazed listening to it. Even after 30 years of doing it over and over again.

The question is: what does it really mean to end suffering? I recall once at ZCLA we were having a workshop on the Four Noble Truths, and Maezumi Roshi was there, and someone said, "I don't get this 'end of suffering.'" There was a story going around at that time. There was a famine in Africa, and a woman who was starving had twins who were starving. And one day she went off in the woods and came back with one baby, because all she could feed was one. And so this woman at the workshop said, "What do you mean no suffering? What about this? How do you answer that?" And no one really answered it. But I think that's the question we all have. Many of us come to this and we hear about the Four Noble Truths, and we think the end of suffering means I'm going to be safe and happy forever. I'll never be sad again. I'm going to find true happiness. But that's spiritual materialism. Chogyam Trongpa was the first one I heard talk about spiritual materialism. It's when I think I'm going to get something out of my spiritual practice. And this "end of suffering" will mean a blissful existence for me. It means God loves me; I will have achieved bliss.

But that's not at all what Buddhist teachings are about. I've been looking at this disconnect, and I've had a couple of things come up that were kind of new to me. Maybe not to you.

When we say the First Noble Truth, life is suffering, what do we mean by life? It's probably our karmic, conditioned life—who our parents are, what our economic situation is, what our health is, what our financial situation is, what our physical appearance is. The conditioned self experiences this life, which is always suffering. Dwelling in the conditional life is suffering. Why? Because it's impermanent. Conditions—karma—are impermanent and always changing. As long as I have my vegan ice cream, I really am in bliss. But then it's gone, and I have a tummy ache. It's constantly changing. We love someone, and then they leave or they die, or we fall out of love.

Our conditional life is a roller coaster. Some people like roller coasters.

TWO ENDS TO SUFFERING

So, this conditional life is suffering, which is our attachment to how things are. We desire things, situations, and relationships, and we suffer. In those attachments, we are ignorant to the true nature of life. So that's a big clue in discovering this end of suffering. Waking up doesn't mean that all of a sudden I become a great person, and only good things happen to me. As we know, bad things happen to good people. Jesus Christ was a good person, right? Look what happened to him.

Yasutani Roshi said that greed, anger and ignorance come from our biology, from our DNA, because just to survive, we need food. My favorite, those brown bears in Alaska—everybody's scared of them, but all they do is eat grass all day. And I went to see those bears, and they paid no attention to me. They were just eating as much as they could. That greed is what keeps them alive. It's what allows them to hibernate. And we also need to protect ourselves and our pack, or tribe. So yeah, if you threaten a bear or their kids, or if you've got food that they want, they can be quite aggressive and kill people, for the sake of survival. Any separation at all is for the sake of survival. That's ignorance, seeing ourselves as separate. My needs, my thoughts, my feelings are separate from yours. And that's part of survival. If I disregard my needs, I'll probably die.

So we're stuck with the three poisons of greed, anger and ignorance, as long as we want to simply survive. So, the way to end suffering is to wake up. And actually, I've been seeing that there are two ways to end suffering.

FULL CIRCLE

One is to wake up to true nature, which is the oneness. To see into the oneness of all things—which is an experience, not a philosophy—has different manifestations. *Samadhi* has different manifestations. *Jijuyu zammai samadhi* is joyous. And then there's *samadhi* of emptiness, just empty. However we experience it, when we do, my needs are just not as important anymore. And your needs become more important to me because you're me and I'm you.

But the other way to end suffering is to do something about the inequality and injustice in the world, to choose to acknowledge the differences and separations, and do something about the harmful ones. There's the suffering of death, which we're all going to face. Well, I had some friends who were trying to be immortal back in the seventies. And they really believed in it. But we will all die. And death is always painful in one way or another. But we can do things to make the process of dying less painful. We have painkillers now and stuff like that, which is nice.

And there is terrible injustice in the world. I just saw this movie about George Foreman. I'm not a boxing fan, but I love biographies. So, I'm watching this biography of George Foreman, and they have this scene where he's little, and his mom is working as a waitress. Basically they have nothing. And they've moved to this horrible place with no electricity and water leaking onto the floor, etc. She's got one McDonald's hamburger—the smallest, cheapest one—and she divides it among her four kids. That kind of suffering we can do something about. No one should struggle in this world, in this

TWO ENDS TO SUFFERING

bountiful world. No one should struggle for food or housing. Buddha said that everyone has the right to sustenance and to be free from insects. Because in India, living out in the open, there are tons of insects. So, there are things we can do in the conditional world to end suffering. And I think maybe that's where we get confused.

From the perspective of oneness, those people are starving—well, it's okay. Everything's one. It's their karma. Suffering is empty. Let them figure it out. But that isn't taking care of our shared life. We can and must do good for others. And it was something my teacher Bernie Glassman Roshi felt very strongly about. He really believed that our practice is useless if we aren't doing something about the terrible suffering of the conditional world.

So, how can we truly wake up to our true nature of oneness—no separation—and also be authentically moved to shift the karmic conditions to end suffering? When we can see for ourselves the emptiness of all things, from that place, our vow becomes to end conditional suffering as well as spiritual suffering.

Shifting karma. After I received transmission, I just started to feel like my life became all about moving the prayer wheel. There was this one huge prayer wheel in Japan, and it took a lot of people to move it around. It was heavy to move. And I started to really get how hard it is to shift karma. It's like that image of rolling a boulder uphill. You get it halfway up and then it rolls down. Then you just start rolling it again. That's the life of the Bodhisattva vowing to shift karma, to change the greed, anger and ignorance that is destroying our world. Often, how to do that is in little teeny ways. Some people have an opportunity to do it in a big way, like politicians have an opportunity to do it in a big way. But for most of us, it is just being kind, following the Precepts.

I also recently watched this biopic about Andy Warhol, who I just really admire as an artist. I love his art, but he suffered so much. He was an unattractive, gay, shy man. And that was hard for him. Then he got shot by someone who supposedly loved him—well, had once loved him but later changed—Valerie Solanas, who wrote the SCUM manifesto on patriarchy. It was supposed to be a kind of performance art when she shot him. I don't know. You may have your opinion, but it was horrendous what happened to him. He was in constant pain for the rest of his life. And he started getting into New Age stuff to feel better. They had interviewed Shirley MacLaine, and she said what they were doing was looking for a practice through which they could be enlightened without suffering. Just wake up to bliss and continue on, blissful forever.

Sure, let's continue to live our privileged life of wealth, leisure, classism, racism, and achieve our bliss in the midst of the great suffering of the world. (That's me being sarcastic). No, Buddhism is very clear—we must experience the suffering in order to end it for the sake of all beings. Ending suffering is not a matter of not feeling negative or painful things. That's why the *Gate of Sweet Nectar* that we chanted this morning says, "being one with the unconditioned Tathagata." Be your life, which

TWO ENDS TO SUFFERING

is also being one with the *conditional* Tathagata. Zazen is about going there, going into who I am, my feelings, my errors, my thoughts, my joy, my me, me, me. Really get to know that little grasping me, in order to let it go, for the sake of others.

Ending suffering is the practice of total immersion into our suffering. That is the path to spiritual awakening, to be who we truly are. That is the way to get to know how we work, and how to do the shifting that loosens up the ego and its attachments.

I'm thinking a lot about shifting karma lately, because nowadays I'm not sitting so much. But being one with that unconditional true self is a big part of ending suffering. And what we do in Zen meditation, a lot of meditation, is cultivate our intimacy with that true self. Essential to the Buddha Way is developing *samadhi*, awakening to the oneness of all things. Let go of the self; experience no-self. And the best way I know to do that is zazen.

Awakening to no-self doesn't mean that we never again conceive of a self or follow karma or have desires. We just come to know what those are, intimately. And we know for sure that their nature is empty. So, I'm really happy all of you are continuing strong sitting practice here, and that you are continuing the other practices of living and working together. That's wisdom work—living together, playing together, practicing the Precepts, doing the right thing, practicing mindfulness in every moment. Not just when you're sitting, but every moment, be aware of what's going on, within and without. Intensive Zen practice is the perfect way to practice the Eightfold Path. It's very hard. It's like rolling the boulder up the hill, because we don't want to do it. We want to go for ice cream and read novels or hang out with our friends. To make the effort to follow the temple schedule is itself the act of the Bodhisattva, to wake up to no suffering.

THE DELUSION OF PRACTICE

I want to acknowledge that ango starts up again on Tuesday. I think this is the first time we've done this—starting ango and then stopping for Christmas and New Years. Hopefully most of us had some fun during the break. For me, a lot of dog parties. And now bam, back into ango. So, I'm kind of psyching myself up. Kosei is the head trainee for this 2-part ango. Thank you, Kosei, very much for holding the space for the rest of us.

I got to thinking about delusion because we use that word all the time. And because the Precept yesterday was *not being deluded*. But what is that? In this day and age, there's so much polarity, and I think a lot of it is due to greed and politics and people telling lies. We really believe that it's *other* people that are deluded. Take vaccinations, for example, which I am definitely in favor of on all fronts. I have no question in my mind about that. And I think people who aren't getting vaccinations are nuts! On the other hand, I have three good friends who feel equally adamant about *not* getting the vaccine. So which one is deluded? It's kind of like that movie,

The Matrix. The first one just blew my mind. I almost had to leave because I got so claustrophobic.

But I recently watched this most recent *Matrix*, and it got me thinking—maybe I am the one that's deluded. Maybe I am the one on the blue pill, and what I believe is real isn't. So what is delusion and how do you tell? In Buddhism, we say we're "ending" delusion. Last night I had trouble sleeping, thinking about it. And then it came to me that getting caught up in deciphering what delusion is or isn't—that for sure is delusion. So, investigating how we talk about delusion, I picked this koan, which is one of the classic koans that you hear over and over again. It's case 19 in *The Gateless Gate (Mumonkan)*:

ORDINARY MIND IS THE WAY

Joshu earnestly asked Nansen, "What is the way?"

Nansen said, "Ordinary mind is the way."

Joshu asked, "Should I direct myself towards it or away from it?"

Nansen said, "If you try to turn towards it, you go against it."

Joshu said, "If I do not try to turn toward it, how can I know that is the way?"

Nansen answered, "The way does not belong to knowing or not knowing. Knowing is delusion. Not knowing is a blank consciousness. When you

THE DELUSION OF PRACTICE

have really reached the true way beyond all doubt, you'll find it is vast and boundless as outer space. How can it be talked about on a level of right and wrong?"

At these words, Joshu was suddenly enlightened.

Joshu was a student of Nansen. In this koan, Joshu's talking to his teacher, one of the great, iconic Chinese Zen masters. Joshu's lineage actually died out, but he's also considered one of the greatest koan masters of all time. And—you are going to be so impressed—I got this book, *The Princeton Dictionary of Buddhism*. Look at that. I have that! It was put together by Robert Buswell and Donald Lopez, both of whom are scholars I know from the Kuroda Institute. And it has everything in here, all you have to do is read the whole thing. But one thing I stumbled across that fascinated me, is this thing called *Kanhua*, which is attributed to Joshu. Kanhua Chan is the practice of "questioning meditation." In a way, this is the essence of Koan practice.

Joshu's most famous koan is *mu*, which some of you are working with. I'll paraphrase it: A monk asked Joshu, "Does that dog have Buddha nature?" And we all know Intellectually—everything is Buddha nature. So of course a dog is Buddha nature! But Joshu says, "*mu*", which essentially means "no", or "none." That's the koan, and it makes you crazy, right? It makes your mind spin, it confuses and frustrates the mind because it's not intellectually clear or graspable. And that's the point of this Kanhua Chan, questioning meditation.

FULL CIRCLE

So why did he say no, *mu*? What is *mu*? Some use the word "taste" in examining what Joshu might have meant. Practicing *mu*, we taste the inability of the unenlightened mind to understand Joshu's motive in giving this response to the question. It raises deep doubt. And doubt makes the mind puzzled, frustrated, and tasteless.

Someone in a recent Council was talking about confusion. Confusion itself is also puzzled, frustrated, tasteless. But that confusion indicates that there's doubt. And that doubt is the inability of the mind to grasp. So, what a wonderful opportunity to practice, to have that doubt arise. Now, for it to work, there also has to be a basis of faith. And that points to the "Three Pillars of Zen": faith, doubt, determination. So the faith is—there *is* an enlightened mind. The faith is that what Buddha said, what the ancestors said, what your teacher says is true. If you don't have that, you're not going to be doing much sitting. Cynicism is not very effective for Zen practice, and I tend to be cynical. So I struggle with Zen practice. But having faith that there is an enlightened mind is the Bodhi Mind. There *is* an enlightened mind, and I have it. Everybody has it. And then, allow the doubt to arise.

What was Joshu talking about? He's like one of the greatest Zen masters of all time, and he's saying nonsense. A child would know that was nonsense. Don and Robert say, "It's as tasteless as chewing on an iron bar." When it's time for supper and what you get is an iron bar, that's how this tastes to the unenlightened mind. It's puzzled, it's frustrated, it's confused. And it doesn't get what Joshu's talking about.

THE DELUSION OF PRACTICE

So, we sit with that. We do zazen—the most important component for Zen Buddhists, for waking up, is zazen, meditation. That's the point of doing ango. Do I move towards it? According to Nansen, there's nothing to move towards. So, what do I do? Sit with that. What is *mu*? What is it? After a while, intellectually, it loses its taste. It becomes flat, becomes awful. And that's the point. We will be moved when that shift happens, when the mind is freed from conceptualization. We kind of wear it out. We get so sick of it, according to this Kanhua Chan practice. And that frees the mind, which leads to liberation.

This is maybe why Joshu's *mu* is so amazing—because it so simply states that process of letting go. I remember being frustrated with *mu*. I was in this little room stuffing cushions, the kapok was flying around. It was a bathroom, I think. And I was just banging my head against the wall about *mu*. What could it be? And then I thought to myself, "Wow, this is just like what a Zen person would do."

Going back to the original koan with Nansen and Joshu—the Joshu who gave us all this stuff I just told you about. This is when he's young, when he's just starting to practice, he hasn't really seen through that frustration, confusion, doubt. And he asks Nansen, "What is the way?" Ordinary mind is the way—just this. Okay, but I don't see that. My ordinary mind is frustrated, confused, afraid. So, Joshu says, "Well, what should I do? Should I direct myself toward it or not?" Should I sit with it? Should I make the effort to get enlightened? Should I do ango? Should I set myself some kind of schedule or not? And Nansen says, "If you try, you go against it." So, by trying, I'm saying I'm not enlightened. I'm trying to be different from who I already am. And that's not it. That's the big joke. That's why, many times, when people have an opening experience, they laugh or cry. Either one. We laugh because, "Oh my God, all along I was it. How silly."

My niece and nephew are all grown up, but when they were little and they did something that was wrong, my sister and brother-in-law wouldn't say, "Don't do that, that's bad," or whatever. They'd say, "That's silly!" And I thought, "What a silly way to raise children." But through my Zen practice, I saw the wisdom in that, "Oh my God. It is silly!" It's just silly to try to get enlightened, because we already are. Ordinary life, this life as it is, without anything extra, this life as it is, is the enlightened life.

But then Joshu says, "If I do not try to turn towards it, how can I know that it is the way?" If I don't have to practice, I can just go to the beach, I can just have fun. Why do I have to do ango? Which, trust me, for anyone who hasn't done ango practice, it's hard, it's rough, and it involves a lot of discipline. Why should I do that? Why should I put myself through that rigorous schedule and abandon so many other aspects of my life? Good question! And Nansen says, "The way is not about knowing or not knowing." It's not about understanding or not understanding. Maybe that's a better way to say that. Just this. "When you have really reached the true way beyond all doubt, you'll find it as vast and boundless as outer space. How can it be talked about on a level of

THE DELUSION OF PRACTICE

right and wrong? At these words Joshu was enlightened." That was Joshu's enlightenment experience.

So, we engage in the delusion of practice, we try to get it. We try with all our might to see what *mu* is, to awaken our enlightened mind. We have faith in the truth of what the Buddhas and Ancestors found out— the oneness of all things, the vastness. We have faith in that. And then that arises the doubt, the frustration, the puzzlement, the tastelessness in practice. What is that? Kanhua, questioning meditation. The meditation of questioning. All the koans are a part of questioning meditation. All that effort; ango is effort, an effort I highly recommend for everyone.

And some of you are brand new to Zen, and you're probably like, "Whoa, I just wanted to come listen to a talk. I don't want to hear about this discipline and dedicated effort." But even if you're brand new, during this period of ango, just sit once a week with the group. Sitting with a group has many benefits. One of them is simply energetic. And I even find that to be true on Zoom, which is weird. Sitting together supports practice and deepens zazen. Just a small, reasonable commitment helps to support that fundamental vow, that deep vow to realize The Way, which is nothing but this ordinary mind. But to realize that is completely different from almost anything else we do.

In Zen, we're training the mind. Like I'm trying to train mine to learn Spanish. We're learning all sorts of things with our unenlightened mind. We're separating, hating, making bad decisions based on greed, anger and ignorance. Ignorance is not realizing our inherently awakened mind. So, little by little, practice to discover that. It is already who you are, and you already have that Bodhi Mind because you're here, showing up for a dharma talk. So just sit, turning toward nothing, with the intention to cultivate your awakened mind.

EFFORT & MIRROR I

I recently read this article in the *New York Times* from a psychologist that said that boredom is really good, because boredom makes us do something. And then it said—nobody likes to just sit still for 10 minutes. But I don't know if that's true. There are lots of people who go to the beach and sit and look out at the ocean for 10 minutes very happily. There are people who enjoy sitting and looking at the stars in the sky. But either way, it is true—we scurry around like little mice. Because we're bored, we come up with stuff to do, and we use up all our resources making more and better stuff.

For Zen practitioners, of course, sitting still is the primary activity. And boredom is certainly a part of sesshin practice. Endless attachments and preferences arise during sesshin. It is a rich field. I was interested to read some of what Dogen Zenji wrote about intensive sitting, so I picked up *The King of Samadhi*. In it, he talks about rising above all the regular people. I almost feel uncomfortable talking about it, because it seems so dualistic and judgmental. We trust Dogen knew what he was doing, but this fascicle boasts a lot of grandeur and magnificence around our practice. It almost sounds like the *Lotus Sutra*, with all of its flower petals and magical beings.

It can be a magical adventure to go into our consciousness, and into our shadows. Exploration is not just something that happens externally. No doubt, we'll always have to scurry about with our little gadgets, running around spending money on external adventures. But as far as the boundless expedition within, I don't believe there is a better way to do that than sesshin. We just sit down and watch what comes up. Hold onto your hats!

Dogen gives great commentary on this one koan that features Reverend Ma, who is also known as Matsuo Baso, a famous Zen master. Some say he's the first person who used the word *Cha'an* Buddhism. Another character in the koan is Nangaku, who I guess is a successor of the Sixth Ancestor, Hui Neng. So, Nangaku is the teacher in this story, and Baso is Nangaku's student. I'll give a quick summary and we can hear it in more detail later. But basically, one day, Baso was sitting in zazen, and Nangaku came over, grabbed a tile and sat facing him, rubbing the tile. Baso asked, "What are you doing?" And Nangaku says, "I'm rubbing the tile to make it a mirror." Baso said, "How can you make a mirror by rubbing a tile?" Nangaku said, "If I can't make a mirror by rubbing a tile, how can you achieve Buddhahood by sitting in meditation?"

How can you achieve Buddhahood by sitting in meditation? The standard way we look at this is, of course, as you are is Buddha. True self, no-self, one body, enlightenment—however you want to say it—that's what you are, inherently. It doesn't have anything to do with sitting or lying down or walking. It's just the truth. So, if we're all Buddha already, then why do we sit? We sit because we don't see it, which only you can determine on your own. It's pretty simple, really. If we can just be quiet within ourselves, and realize how we're holding on to all of our ideas and agendas, we'll see it. That's one way to understand this "polishing of a tile" comment.

But I really wanted to talk about Dogen's commentary on this story from the *Shobogenzo*. He starts by pointing out that Nangaku had already given the mind-seal to Baso, just before this story took place. The mind-seal is the teacher's acknowledgement that "you have my mind," which is the mind of the Buddha, which has been transmitted and handed down from Shakyamuni. But this story ends in Baso's "Great Enlightenment." So, it seems he received transmission before his "Great Enlightenment," which happens. Dogen's "Great Enlightenment" apparently happened after he received transmission from his Rinzai teacher. Even though he'd received transmission, he wasn't satisfied. So he went to China and had his huge opening there, when he said that body and mind had completely dropped off. And, of course, there is no ultimate experience or understanding. There is no end point to practice. There's always more.

Back to the story—Baso had been doing seated meditation day in and day out for some 10 years or more. For me, I believe it was 15 years of full time sitting before I had transmission. So much sitting. Why did I do that? I actually only once questioned my commitment—in 1982, when there was trouble at the Zen Center. I stopped sitting for a month, and very quickly noticed how much I missed it. My life was just different, so I went back to daily zazen.

We do have one story of awakening in our lineage that didn't involve long periods of intensive practice, and that's the story of Hui Neng, the Sixth Ancestor. Apparently, he awakened by hearing the Diamond Sutra recited in the streets of his village. But then that awakening experience drove him to intensive monastic practice for the rest of his life. So, 10 years is actually a pretty short amount of time in the context of our lifelong practice.

So, Baso had been sitting for 10 years in this thatched hut. Imagine what that was like on a rainy night. Even when his hut was covered in snow, he never left from that freezing floor. No matter what, he kept at it for 10 years. And one day Nangaku came to Baso said,

> *"What have you been doing recently?"*
>
> *"Recently I have been doing the practice of seated meditation exclusively."*
>
> *"And what is the aim of your seated meditation?"*
>
> *"The aim of my seated meditation is to achieve Buddhahood."*

One practice of the Eightfold Path is Right

EFFORT & MIRROR I

Effort—giving our best effort to let go of greed, anger, and ignorance, opening up to compassion, wisdom and spaciousness. Also, one of the *Paramitas* is Joyous Effort. Or, *Verya Paramita*. We practice this *paramita* in sesshin practice. We just keep on going, following the schedule, for the sake of liberation for all beings. Disillusionment comes up, wishing we were somewhere else, feeling stale in our sitting. And then that must be where we focus our effort. What is that disillusionment? What else am I looking for? What's wrong with just this?

The Buddha experienced that too. After he decided to not move from the Bodhi Tree until he was truly satisfied in his awakening, the evil demon Mara tried to tempt him away from that single-minded effort. He sent beautiful women to seduce him. He conjured images of his family begging him to come back, because they were in trouble. It was cold; birds made a nest in his hair. Imagine how many bugs were crawling all over him—so many reasons to get up and do something else. But that unwavering effort kept him there.

So, in the story, Nangaku asks Baso, "What are you striving for? All you do is seated meditation, for 10 years. What is your aim?" And Baso says that the aim is to achieve Buddhahood. But once we start getting into aim, we're already lost in dualistic understanding. The deepest effort is to practice just for the sake of practicing. So, here is where Nangaku took the roof tile and began rubbing it. And Baso says,

"What are you going to make by polishing a roof

tile?"

"I am polishing it to make a mirror."

"How can you possibly make a mirror by rubbing a tile?"

"How can you possibly make yourself into a Buddha by doing seated meditation?"

A roof tile is Buddha. Everything is Buddha. So polishing a tile to make a mirror makes as much sense as sitting to become Buddha. And the word "mirror" has a much bigger implication in Buddhism. We can see all of life as a mirror, an expression of our consciousness, our true self. A mirror reflects everything perfectly. So, to say that the roof tile is a mirror, in a way, is exactly what it is. The true nature of everything is to be a mirror of the universe. And our delusion, all our ideas and concepts we have built up over years and years of karmic existence, distort that perfect image reflected in the universal mirror.

There's nothing special about this tile; it's just an ordinary household item. I see him sitting in the woods, near a structure that a tile has fallen off of. It could have been a stone or a leaf; it could have been anything. In fact, in order for his teaching to get across, it had to be something particularly ordinary and of the moment. Awakening is seeing the ordinary and extraordinary as one. That's why boredom is so important in zazen. If we can experience boundless oneness, even in the midst of boredom, then we're free. Any ordinary moment or

EFFORT & MIRROR I

object is a mirror that reflects the whole universe.

None of this can be explained well. It's just pathetic how I'm talking about it. Dogen does the most magnificent job of all, but still doesn't get close to touching it. In his commentary he says,

> *We should truly comprehend that when the polished tile became a mirror, Baso became a Buddha.*

It was a mirror all along. But we must experience that shift, when everything becomes a mirror and we become Buddha.

> *And when Baso became Buddha, Baso immediately became the real Baso. And when Baso became the real Baso, his sitting in meditation immediately became real seated meditation. This is why the saying, "polishing a tile to make a mirror" has been preserved in the bones and marrow of former Buddhas.*

This I love. When you sit, you become the real you.

I was talking with someone recently about what *shikantaza* is. Sometimes, what people call *shikantaza* is more like what we think of as mindfulness. But they are, in fact, quite different. In *shikantaza*, there is no object of meditation, no meditation at all. And I recall Yasutani Roshi saying in *The Three Pillars of Zen* that when you really do *shikantaza*, you should be sweating from every pore of your body. *Shikantaza* is the direct practice of *samadhi*. Mindfulness is also an important aspect of The Eightfold Path—being aware of sensations, breath, emotions, etc. But there is still a focus, an object there. In *shikantaza*, there are no sensations, no breath, no emotions.

That's Dogen Zenji's experience of "dropping off body and mind." As the *Maha Prajna Paramita Heart Sutra* says, "No eye, ear, nose, tongue, body, mind . . ." *Shikantaza* is being totally lost in awareness, with no awareness of awareness. That's my best attempt at explaining, but really, I don't know what *shikantaza* is. But "When Baso became the real Baso, his sitting in meditation immediately became real seated meditation." And that's what we struggle to define—what is real seated meditation? What I can say is that it definitely includes boredom. It includes everything.

The first part of Right Effort is the vow to awaken. So, when I start hurting, or get bored, or am confronted by my shadow, it's so easy to want to escape to my happy place. That could be a fantasy place, or it could be that joyful, peaceful period of zazen I had before—anything but feeling this fear, this anger, this regret, this jealousy. But just stay with what's coming up. That's the real you, in real seated meditation. Be with it, without holding onto it. Be willing to let it go, which is very different from avoiding it or repressing it.

So, when we sit, we polish a tile and make a mirror of it. We achieve Buddhahood when our meditation is real meditation. And that real meditation is where we get to see our true self reflected in absolutely everything. I appreciate your practice and your effort, your devotion, and your willingness to persevere in the face of disillusionment. And if you are unclear about what real meditation is, or why you are even persevering like this, then you're probably onto something.

EFFORT & MIRROR II

We just finished a week-long sesshin, which always seems like a month. A whole week of zazen, tons of meditation, and no matter how many times I do it, it never ceases to be astonishing. It's probably the hardest thing that I do. And it's also my favorite thing I do.

I wanted to expand a bit upon the story about Nangaku and Baso, and polishing a tile. I'm always amazed by how old some of these stories are. This one's probably over a thousand years old. Nangaku is the Sixth Ancestors' successor. And Baso is Nangaku's successor.

Recall, Nangaku asks Baso, "Why are you doing so much zazen?" And that's probably a question that comes up for a lot of us during sesshin. Why spend a whole week in silence, investigating every breath, every moment? And then we probably have resistance—this is stupid, think of all the other things I could be doing. But that resistance is a treasure trove. What is that resistance? Whose is it? That resistance itself is one of the most important gateways we can enter on our spiritual journey.

FULL CIRCLE

Baso responds, "My aim is to achieve Buddhahood." But, of course, to think of achieving anything transgresses the great emptiness of the universe. So, poor Baso is working so hard when, really, there's nothing to do. As you are is Buddha. All of this zazen, *dokusan*,[5] chanting—all of the trappings of Buddhist practice—if we're doing it to become something called a Buddha, we're likely to be disappointed. But if we're doing it to manifest our most authentic, true self, then we honor all the Buddhas and ancestors.

Dogen's commentary on this case is from a fascicle called *Kokyo*, from his great work *Shobogenzo*.

> *Be very clear about it. The functioning of the true transmission of Buddhists and ancestors involves direct pointing.*

A good teacher points to something directly. Nangaku rubs the tile to make a mirror. This mirror, this ancient mirror, is our true self. When everything is one, where could you possibly not be reflected perfectly? Common sense tells us that you can't make a mirror from a tile. But Dogen says, of course you can do that! The nature of the tile *is* a mirror. My nature is a mirror. Your nature is a mirror. Just don't forget the wisdom of the Sixth Ancestor—the mirror has no stand.

When we experience "dropped off body and mind," we experience our true self. Sit with who you are. Don't try to be someone else. And if you do that, you will see clearly that what you are is fully enlightened, as you

EFFORT & MIRROR II

are right now. For some people, they can sit once and have that experience right away. And for some of us it takes years and lifetimes of practice. I know some people who have never meditated and yet seem to behave from that kind of understanding. We all have our path. And really, *daikensho* (Great Awakening) goes on forever, deepens forever. It's not a one-off experience and then you're done. That must get dropped off too.

I wanted to tell you a story about Steve, my next door neighbor, who is also my dog Bruno's best friend. Steve is retired, but he was a medic in the fire department. Medics basically do the same thing the firefighters do. Apparently, there's a lot of time just waiting in the station house all the time. So they have a lot of time with not much to do, hopefully. So, according to Steve, what they do is clean. They clean all the time. And Steve, bless his heart, is probably over there right now polishing his car. He's got an ATV, he's got a truck, he's got a car, and he's got a patio. So, anytime you go over there, he's polishing. I went over there yesterday and he was polishing his ATV, and man—it just shines. It seems like all day long, he's polishing. And he's so sweet, he doesn't judge you if your stuff isn't so polished. But he will acknowledge—after I get a carwash or something, he'll say, "Oh, your car looks nice." Some nice encouragement from Steve.

This reminds me of what Dogen is saying, which is that the act of polishing is enlightenment, *because* it's already polished. The mirror is already there. So, polish it. Take care of your life, and of the things you care about. It's a matter of gratitude. Steve polished the firetruck because he's grateful that it puts out fires, that it makes people feel safe.

Dogen said:

> *The very act of polishing is itself the mirror.*
> *Buddha polishing Buddha. Enlightenment*
> *polishing enlightenment.*

Polishing is enlightenment. And so, to say, "We don't need to put forth so much effort to sit, because we're already Buddha," totally misses the point. It's *because* I'm enlightened that I sit. Because it's beautiful and clean and perfect, we polish it. And to do zazen is the act of polishing what is already a perfect mirror. We sit to enjoy ourselves, to appreciate ourselves, and to know our true self, which is not separate from anything.

Please take a look at this fascicle on your own. It's called *Kokyo*, which means "ancient mirror". It was never born; it's that old; it will never die. It's the all-inclusive mirror that reflects everything perfectly. Even just talking about this image of polishing—I think I'm going to start being better at keeping things clean. I'm feeling a lot of appreciation for Steve and his polishing. Don't let your perfection make you complacent. We polish, we do zazen, and we serve others. Grab a tile.

YOUR INGREDIENTS I

I love doing the Fusatsu ceremony on New Years Eve. We do Fusatsu every month, around the full moon, reflecting on our conduct and practice over the previous month. So, this is the big one, when we can reflect on the whole year and then, let it go. Dogen said that remembering past lives is bad karma. And I always took that to mean that remembering the past, in general, is bad karma—dwelling and attaching. But he also talked about how important it is to acknowledge cause and effect. When we do something that we could have done better, when we make a mistake, when we do something great, when we hurt someone else, when we help someone else etc., we should acknowledge it, atone when appropriate, and then let it go. That's a primary aspect of Fusatsu, atonement. So, this is a time for deep reflection; a good time to sit.

I wanted to talk about Dogen Zenji's classic work, *Instructions To The Cook (Tenzo Kyokun)*. Uchiyama Roshi wrote a lot of commentary on the *Tenzo Kyokun*, which he turned into a collection he named *How To Cook Your*

Life. I recently realized that I haven't talked much at all about the *Tenzo Kyokun*. It was one of Maezumi Roshi's favorite texts to talk about. He went through it twice with us, giving dharma talks paragraph by paragraph, and it took a long time. When I look at it now, I really see how good it is. For those of you who would like to study Dogen, *Tenzo Kyokun* offers a very accessible opportunity to read his teachings. Some of Dogen is really difficult to untangle, partially because he wrote in ancient Japanese, which is like us reading Old English—*Beowulf* or something. So, translating Dogen is hard because the language is ancient. And his use of language is exquisite. He wrung every possible drop of juice out of his words. And then of course, it's hard to translate and grasp the puns and wordplay of those days. We're so fortunate to have some really excellent translators of Dogen's works.

The *tenzo* is the cook in the monastery. Many Zen Centers and temples have a *tenzo*. Zen Center of Los Angeles and Yokoji Zen Mountain Center, our mother temples, have often had a regular *tenzo* as an official position. Many American practice centers have modeled their staff and personnel after the traditional Japanese monastery positions. There's the *ino*, who facilitates the ceremony and ritual for the Sangha. There's the *fusu*, or treasurer, who manages the finances. The abbot oversees pretty much everything. But the *tenzo* is a very high-ranking, important position, which partly comes out of these Dogen talks about the importance of the *tenzo*.

YOUR INGREDIENTS I

He talks about three kinds of minds that make up the *tenzo* mind. The first is a joyful mind.

> *A joyful spirit is one of gratefulness and buoyancy. You should consider this carefully. If you have been born into some heavenly realm, you would most likely have only become attached to the pleasures, taking neither time nor opportunity to awaken the Bodhi spirit. Nor would you be likely to feel any particular necessity for practicing the Buddha Dharma. Much less would you be able to prepare meals for the Three Treasures, despite they're being the highest and most worthy of things. Therefore, rejoice in your birth into the world where you are capable of using your body freely, to offer food to the Three Treasures. Considering the innumerable possibilities of a timeless universe, we have been given a marvelous opportunity. The merit of working as a tenzo will never decay. My sincerest desire is that you exhaust all the strength and effort of all your lives past, present, and future, and every moment of every day into your practice, through the work of the tenzo, so that you form a strong connection with the Buddhadharma. To view all things with this attitude is called joyful mind.*

Rejoice that we are fortunate enough to be born into a situation where we can encounter the *Buddhadharma*. It's our great fortune to encounter it and to actually practice it! And he particularly praises the practice of the cook. The first part of the book is mostly on how to be mindful, how to treat every leaf of lettuce as Buddha, how to see the holiness in every ingredient and in the serving of food. When I was *tenzo*, I spent a lot of time crying because it was hard work, and people had a lot of opinions about food. It's a hard job. So, how can we cultivate gratitude and joyful mind in every challenging situation in our life?

> *The deeds of even a benevolent ruler disappear quickly, like foam or water, or the windblown flame of a candle. Rather than be such a ruler, it would be of more value to the Buddhadharma for you to prepare meals and offer them to the Three Treasures.*

When I was *tenzo*, my mother was upset because she felt like, "I didn't raise you to be a cook, cooking for other people." But in our tradition, the cook is seen as one of the most valuable, most respectable jobs.

The second mind Dogen talks about is the mind of a parent.

> *In the way that a parent cares for an only child, keep the Three Treasures in your mind. A parent, irrespective of poverty for difficult circumstances, loves and raises a child with care. How deep is love like this? Only a parent can understand it. A parent protects the children from the cold and shades them from the hot sun, with no concern for their own personal welfare. Only a person in whom this mind has arisen can understand it. And only one in whom*

> *this attitude has become second nature can fully realize it. This is the ultimate in being a parent. In this same manner, when you handle water, rice or anything else, you must have the affectionate and caring concern of a parent raising a child.*

I remember once Ram Dass was visiting Bernie, and I had the good fortune to be there. And there was this old, mangy dog. Ram Dass took that dog's head in his hands, and talked so much love to it, "You're so beautiful, you're so wonderful." It was very sweet. Ram Dass was like that. He gave an outpouring of love to whatever he encountered. So, hold everything as a parent to it—the food, the bowl, the utensils we eat with, the broom etc.

Dogen goes on to say:

> *Shakyamuni took 20 years off his life expectancy to care for us in later generations. The significance of this was simply a demonstration of parental mind. The Tathagata did not do this with an expectation of some reward or fame. He did it unconditionally without thought of profit or gain.*

And then the third mind is magnanimous mind.

> *Magnanimous mind is like a mountain, stable and impartial, exemplifying the ocean. It is tolerant, and views everything from the broadest perspective. Having a magnanimous mind means being without prejudice and refusing to take sides. When carrying something that weighs an ounce, do not think of*

it as light. And likewise, when you have to carry 50 pounds, do not think of it as heavy. Do not get carried away by the sounds of spring nor become heavy hearted upon seeing the colors of fall. View the changes of the seasons as a whole, and weigh the relativeness of light and heavy from a broad perspective. It is then that you should write, understand, and study the character for magnanimous.

Of course, it's important to recognize good and bad. But the thing is, our mind can get stuck in its ideas of good and bad. My mind is always judging and comparing, "This is good; that is bad." I feel like I'm just now really getting in touch with how much of the stress in my body comes from my constant judgment. So, cultivate this magnanimous mind—total tolerance, not taking sides. And then, of course, when we witness clearly harmful behavior, we must stand up and take action. But that action is so much more powerful when it comes from a magnanimous mind, instead of a judgmental, intolerant mind.

Roshi Bernie wrote a commentary on the *Tenzo Kyokun* as well, which is called, *Instructions to the Cook*. He wrote it with Rick Fields, who's gone now. It's another book that's really worth reading for a couple of reasons. One is his understanding of the *Tenzo Kyokun*. But it also gives you a very intimate view of Bernie himself. He and Roshi, Jisho Holmes put together the Three Tenets, which have become a major teaching of our lineage. The Three Tenets are:

YOUR INGREDIENTS I

1) Not-Knowing
2) Bearing Witness
3) Loving Action

Dogen is basically talking about them, using his own language. It may seem like he's writing about cooking. But this "magnanimous mind" is essentially Not-Knowing. It is the empty mind, free of judgment. He also goes into detail about Bearing Witness—to our ingredients, to what is here in this moment, whatever life has offered us.

In his book, Bernie talks about the ingredients of our life. You open up the refrigerator and there's half a cup of beans, a little rice, a carrot, a potato, maybe some mushrooms. Do you regret that you don't have other ingredients? Or do you just try to make the very best meal out of what's in your refrigerator right now? Each of us has a unique set of ingredients, which you can call karma. We're different sizes, we have different skills and flaws, we have different kinds of families that are given incredibly different circumstances. And we suffer when we start judging those differences—it's so lucky to have been born into a wealthy family, it's so sad to have been born in a poor little town in Mexico. Our practice is about dropping the judgment and doing what's appropriate with the ingredients we're given. As you know, there are many wealthy people who have terrible lives, and there are many wonderful, thriving people who live in humble situations.

From this kind of awareness, judgment doesn't make much sense. Why should I be jealous of your ingredients when I've got all of mine to deal with? So, the Bearing Witness aspect of the *Tenzo Kyokun* is the practice of being intimate with what our ingredients are. Before preparing the meal, the *tenzo* measures how much rice there is, and how many vegetables. Then, based on that Bearing Witness, they can prepare the meal. And that's the third of the Three Tenets—Loving Action. So, from that joyful mind of Not-Knowing, and as we bear witness to our ingredients with the spirit of a parent, we allow the best action, or meal, to arise naturally.

Dogen left Japan for China because he wasn't satisfied with his practice in Japan. Everyone thought he was great, but he himself wasn't satisfied with his understanding. I can't tell you how many people come to see me in *dokusan* wanting me to verify or approve their level of understanding or enlightenment. But I really have no idea what your understanding is. I can help provide a container, which is sesshin, and maybe some advice or words of wisdom to support you on your path. But the one who approves your understanding is you. Are *you* satisfied? Do you genuinely see your life as the *Tathagata* itself? Well, Dogen wasn't quite satisfied in Japan, so he decided to go to China to practice with Rujing.

There were many stories involving a *tenzo* on his journey. When Dogen first gets to China, he meets this one *tenzo*, who's shopping at the market. And Dogen says, "Please stay and talk to me. I want to hear more about your practice here" or something. And the *tenzo* says, "No, I've got to go. It's my job to hurry back and cook." Many of us might say it's rude to run off like that. It would be better for the guy to stay and connect with Dogen, and encourage him. But he declines, so that he can focus on his duties as *tenzo*.

Then, Dogen finds himself a monastery in China to practice at, and one day he's walking around and it's very hot.

> *When I was at Mount Tientong, a monk called Liu from Quin Fu was serving as tenzo. One day after the noon meal, I was walking to another building within the complex, when I noticed Liu drying mushrooms in the sun in front of the Buddha Hall. He carried a bamboo stick, but no hat on his head. The sun rays beat down so harshly, that the tiles along the walk burned one's feet. Liu worked hard and was covered with sweat. I could not help but feel the work was too much of a strain for him. His back was a bow drawn taut. His long eyebrows were crane white. I approached and asked his age. He replied that he was 68 years old. Then I went on to ask him why he never used any assistance. He answered, "other people are not me." "You are right," I said, "I can see that your work is the activity of the Buddhadharma, but why are you working so hard in the scorching sun?" Liu replied, "If I do not do it now, when else can I do it?" There was nothing else for me to say. As I walked on along the passageways, I began to sense inwardly the true significance of the role of the tenzo.*

FULL CIRCLE

Please allow me to encourage you to use this time to contemplate all of these things. Invite joyful mind, gratitude, magnanimous mind and the Three Tenets. I was just reading about someone who was thinking of taking their life. Nowadays, oh my goodness, there's so much depression, suicide and drug use. Life is hard. And these past few years, post COVID, have been very hard for everyone. But I recently read something from someone that said that they simply just started writing down the things they're grateful for. So, I started doing that too.

I'm usually pretty joyful. But every once in a while, something catches me, and all of a sudden everything seems wrong—I'm a failure and nothing is ok. But if I take a moment to look out my window and see the ocean, to see my dogs and all of you here, to acknowledge all of your efforts to practice and take care of the Zen center, after a while, I can regain that appreciation for my ingredients. Of course, that doesn't mean we should disregard the pain and grief that we experience. The Three Tenets encourage us to bear witness to the joy AND pain of the universe. So, practicing gratitude doesn't mean ignoring suffering and hardship. It means we see our joys and pains, and everything in-between, as ingredients for us to make the best meal possible.

This Christmas was one of the only times I gave something to all my neighbors and all the workers in the community. It was wonderful. It felt so great and so fun to give presents. I'm not a parent, I just have dogs. But I see that joy of giving in those of you who are parents. It's Buddha action to open up that parental mind of caring

YOUR INGREDIENTS I

for all beings. Practice magnanimous mind; experience no separation. That's how we can really work on our judgment. I really have to work on my judgment. I want to cultivate that magnanimous mind that can feel every moment and every being as full, perfect.

So, let's just keep on going. Another major aspect of the *Tenzo Kyokun* is the importance of constant practice. Everything is practice. So, when you go to make your meal, rather than rushing and throwing something together, invite that appreciation of whatever the ingredients are that are going into the meal. And appreciate yourself and what a wonderful ingredient you are.

YOUR INGREDIENTS II

I'm doing this online training with my dogs, because we've been traveling together and I realized they needed more training. The whole point of the training is to change patterns in both the dogs and the person. And it's really hard work. All three of us are exhausted. We get so easily reliant on our patterns. But we shouldn't because, in fact, things are constantly changing. That's partially why the COVID pandemic was like a worldwide sesshin for everyone. All of a sudden, everyone's pattern was disrupted, and we all struggled with that.

I wanted to keep talking about Dogen's *Tenzo Kyokun*, and Bernie's *Instructions To The Cook*. Yesterday, we talked about the three minds of the *tenzo*—joyful, parental and magnanimous. And we talked about appreciating every ingredient, being mindful of every ingredient.

Dogen says,

> When you prepare food, never view the ingredients from some commonly held perspective, or think

about them only with your emotions. Maintain an attitude that tries to build great temples from ordinary greens, that expounds the Buddhadharma through the most trivial activity. When making a soup with ordinary greens, do not be carried away by feelings or dislike towards them, nor regard them lightly. Neither jump for joy simply because you have been given the ingredients of superior quality to make a special dish. By the same token that you do not indulge in a meal because of its particularly good taste, there is no reason to feel an aversion where it's an ordinary one. Do not be negligent and careless just because the materials seem plain, and hesitate to work more diligently with materials of superior quality. Your attitude towards things should not be contingent upon their quality. A person who is influenced by the quality of a thing, or who changes his speech or manner according to the appearance or position of the people he meets, is not a man working in The Way.

I feel like people often complain about Zen being too boring. We do the same thing every morning: get up, do zazen, do work in the garden, prepare meals, make a spreadsheet, more zazen, go to bed. It's not always glamorous and exciting. And that's what I hear from people about Zen practice. And it's true, intensive Zen practice can be boring. But it can also be too intense and engaging—too many deep emotions flare up, there's too much to look at. And that's true for everyone, at one point or another. We have difficulty when it's too

YOUR INGREDIENTS II

boring, and we have difficulty when it's too dramatic.

But through this practice, we cultivate the ability to see and appreciate everything just as it is in this moment, without judgment. One day it's dramatic and exciting, the next day it's ordinary and boring. That's it! And cultivating that mind is not easy, because we constantly yearn for things to be different. To accept and appreciate things as they are is this gratitude mind Dogen talks about. And Bernie talks about it as accepting our ingredients in each moment. It could be champagne and caviar, could be beans and rice. That's our practice.

Dogen goes on to say:

> These things are truly just a matter of course. Yet we remain unclear about them because our minds go racing about like horses running wild in the fields, while our emotions remain unmanageable, like monkeys swinging in the trees. If only we would step back to carefully reflect on the horse and monkey, our lives would naturally become one with our work. Doing so is the means whereby we turn things, even while simultaneously we are being turned by them.

I've heard people say that about breath. When we start Zen practice, we are breathing. And at some point, we realize we are being breathed. Getting in touch with that is marvelous—to let go of myself thoroughly enough to be fully in accord with the universe.

It is vital that we clarify and harmonize our lives with our work, and not lose sight of either the absolute or the practical. Handle even a single leaf of a green in such a way that it manifests the body of the Buddha. This, in turn, allows the Buddha to manifest through the leaf. This is a power which you cannot grasp with your rational mind. It operates freely according to the situation in the most natural way. At the same time, this power functions in our lives to clarify and settle activity, and is beneficial to all living things.

Just recently, I was sitting in zazen, and not quite comfortable. Then, all of a sudden, a rush of energy just raced through me. My posture straightened, and the discomfort disappeared. I don't know what it was, but this power that you can't grasp with your rational mind arises out of zazen. We can allow ourselves to be clear, and we can deeply settle. But as he says, this is not rational. So, I'll move on.

Dogen received a lot of profound insight from the *tenzos* that he met. I mentioned this particular story yesterday, about when he arrived in China.

I arrived in China in April, 1223, but being unable to disembark immediately, I stayed onboard the ship. One day in May while I was talking with the captain, an old monk about 60 years of age came directly to the ship to buy mushrooms from the Japanese merchants on board. I invited him for tea and asked him where he was from. He said he was the tenzo at the monastery on Mount Ayuwang and added, "I'm originally from Xishu, although I left there over 40 years ago. I am 61 this year and have practiced in several Zen monasteries last year while living in Guyun. I visited the monastery on Mount Ayuwang, though I spent my time there totally confused as to what I was doing. Then, after the summer practice period, I was appointed tenzo. Tomorrow is May 5th, but I have nothing special to offer the monks. I wanted to prepare a noodle soup, but as I did not have any mushrooms to put in it, I came here to buy some."

I asked, "When did you leave Ayuwang?"

He replied, "After lunch."

"Is it far from here?"

"About 14 miles."

"When will you go back?"

"I was planning to return as soon as I bought the mushrooms."

"You can't imagine how fortunate I feel that we were able to meet unexpectedly like this. If it's possible, I wish you would stay a while longer and allow me to offer you something more."

"I'm sorry, but that is impossible just now. If I am not there tomorrow to prepare the meal, it will not be made well."

So, he had walked 14 miles, which could be about five hours, to buy some mushrooms. And then he was headed back to make this special meal for the sangha. So, Dogen goes on:

In July of the same year, I stayed on Mount Tiantong. One day, the tenzo came to see me. He said, "As the summer practice period has ended, I shall be retiring as tenzo and plan to return home. I heard that you were here, and wanted very much to talk with you and see how you were doing."

I was happy to see him. And we talked about many things that finally came to the matter concerning the practice and study of characters. He said, "A person who studies characters must know just what characters are, and one intending to practice The Way must understand what practice is."

I asked him once again, "What are the characters?"

"1, 2, 3, 4, 5." He replied.

"What is practice?"

"There is nothing in the world that is hidden."

The characters, the numbers, our intellectual mind, our discriminating mind—how much time do you spend in your head analyzing things, trying to understand things, naming things, numbering things? And what the *tenzo* says is that true practice is taking care of what's right here. His job is to go home and fix the noodles.

YOUR INGREDIENTS II

So that's what he does. We might think that it's better to stay and share the Dharma with Dogen, but his job is cooking the noodles.

As I said yesterday, I think the *Tenzo Kyokun* is possibly the most accessible of Dogen's writings. So, for those who want to start reading Dogen, I highly recommend it. It's quite easy to see what he's saying—let go of our grasping, our ideas and concepts, and just be in each moment. Which is simply taking care of what needs to be taken care of, whatever our position is.

I wanted to read you the introduction to Bernie Tetsugen Roshi's book, *Instructions To The Cook*, where he talks about how he became inspired to write the book in the first place. This book is great too, especially if you want to get to know Bernie better. It really goes into his move towards social action, the beginnings of the Greyston Bakery, and the root of a lot of his thinking. But here's a bit from the prologue:

> When I first began to study Zen, my teacher, Maezumi Roshi, gave me a koan: "How do you go further from the top of a hundred-foot pole?" You can't use your rational mind to answer this poem, or any Zen question in a logical way. You might meditate a long time and come back to the Zen master and say, "The answer is to live fully."

"How do you step forward from a hundred-foot pole" implies—after waking up to the oneness of all things, to the fact of No-Self, then what? What do you do when you reach the top, the very peak of your practice?

Step off where? Step off how? Bernie says that maybe you say the answer is to live fully.

> *That's a good beginning, but it's only the rational, logical part of the answer. You have to go further. You have to demonstrate the answer. You have to embody the answer. You have to show the Zen master how you live fully in the moment.*

So those of you working on koans with me know that that's what I'll say. How do you show it? How do you demonstrate it? Please don't explain it to me. It has to be from your gut. How do you move from your gut and embody this koan? Koan practice is not intellectual. And it gets harder for those who continue to try to make it intellectual, myself included. It's much easier for a child to do koans, because children embody things more naturally. It's only after we start developing and training our intellect that we start getting so attached to it.

Bernie's intro goes on:

> *You have to manifest the answer in your life, in your everyday relationships, in the marketplace, at work, as well as in the temple, our meditation hall. When we live our life fully, our life becomes what Zen Buddhists call the Supreme Meal. We make the Supreme Meal by using the ingredients at hand to make the best meal possible, then by offering. This book is about how to cook the Supreme Meal of your life. This book is about how to step off a*

YOUR INGREDIENTS II

hundred-foot pole and live fully in the marketplace and in every other sphere of your life.

The marketplace refers to the 10th Ox Herding Picture, which is from an old Zen teaching that represents the "last step" of spiritual practice. And of course, any of these linear stages or steps are really circles that we go around in over and over. But Bernie's referring to the idea that the highest spiritual achievement is to live fully in every moment, to appreciate our life, which Maezumi Roshi always said. It is to appreciate our ingredients, which is that grateful mind Dogen talks about.

Just use the ingredients you have. Don't look around so much—more money, more friends, better Facebook posts, a better understanding, more time to sit, less time to sit. Use what you have right here, right now. Maybe there's an ingredient I can't use now, but I can use it for dessert, or for tomorrow's breakfast. If one of your ingredients has spoiled, then the correct way to use it is to put it in the compost pale. And it's true, some refrigerators are deeply broken, and things spoil to a point where they need special consideration. Sometimes to protect others, we need a revisioning of the recipe.

I've been thinking about transformation lately, because it seems like there's so much of it in American Zen, in my life, in my friends' lives. Every moment is a new moment. So, in every moment, we have the opportunity to completely transform. Every moment, we can choose to look at things in a different way. I remember Tenshin Roshi saying, "If you're knocking your head against the door, trying to get through, turn around. Maybe there's an open door behind you." Transformation means accepting all the ingredients, everything that I have. It means opening up to the shadow, opening up to people we usually wouldn't.

One time, after Bernie had gone to New York, he came back to ZCLA for a visit. I remember a particular conversation we had in the wood shop there. He said to me that he had started the practice of looking at who is excluded. In any group or organization, who's being excluded? There will always be some kind of exclusivity for any group. But to be aware of it can allow us to see how the exclusion causes harm. Looking earnestly at how exclusion shows up for us is how to move further towards healthy inclusion.

My favorite Bernie koan is apparently a real story: people were doing service, and there was a very good looking young priest whose robes were perfect, unlike mine. Everybody looked up to him. He was very fastidious about how service was done. One day, an unhoused person came in and, you know, didn't smell that good. And he was late. He came in after service had started, and the young priest said, "You can't come in here now, the service has already started." And he says, "But Father," as Bernie explained, this unhoused person was Catholic. "Father, I've already taken off my shoes," which to me means "I've already done the first step of opening myself up to the dharma, and you won't let me in. Won't you please let me in?"

Who are we excluding? Sure, holding tardy people accountable can be helpful for a community, in certain

YOUR INGREDIENTS II

circumstances. But when someone new has that genuine aspiration and comes a little late, what do you do?

Going on with Bernie's *Instructions To The Cook*, he's very interested in keeping things clean and orderly, which I didn't know. I never heard him talk about that, but wow, that's a good practice. I have a lot of clutter. I'm going to think about that. It's like I keep things around because I feel like something's missing. But what? Nothing is missing. I have all my ingredients. I'm not young; I'm not beautiful; I'm not rich. This is who I am. When we encounter our faults, and find ourselves doing something that goes against our values, that's a wonderful point of practice. We all know that dark place that has no joy, no gratitude. It is filled with guilt or blame, or depression. And that is such fertile ground for practice. That place feels awful. "I liked it when I was happy. I hate this. Life sucks."

And then this little voice goes, "Just be it." How we work with our faults, how we show up in that rabbit hole of darkness, that is the functioning of our practice.

Many Zen temples, like ours, don't use *tenzos* anymore. And I really like that we all act as our own *tenzo* during sesshin. It's important to honor dietary needs, for our health and wellbeing. Though, it is a wonderful practice when we have an opportunity to prepare and serve food for others. Whatever you're doing, completely embody your work, and treat it as service. Then you will enjoy it. Let's keep on going!

PRECEPT BEINGS

I asked to do Fusatsu today, during sesshin—silent retreat—because this moon is so beautiful. I guess it's always beautiful. But when I see the full moon, I always think, "Well, it's Fusatsu!" This is our time to reflect on our lives together. Fusatsu is an ancient practice from the time of the Buddha. Isn't that amazing? All those years of people doing zazen and Fusatsu together. So, we decided to do it during sesshin, which may be a first for us. The Precept we're looking at this month is the 5th of the 10 Bodhisattva Precepts:

Not being deluded nor encouraging others to do so. I will cultivate a mind that sees clearly, I will embrace all experience directly.

This can refer to intoxicants, like drugs and alcohol, but it also includes all the ways we try to escape facing this moment. I had about half a chocolate bar earlier because I was nervous about the dogs. It was delicious. As a former biochemist, (a very short-term biochemist),

FULL CIRCLE

I worked on evolution in biochemistry. I'm a believer in examining our behavior from the standpoint of our biochemistry driving us to do stuff. For example, we have chemicals in us that compel us to have babies. In a way, our only job is to have and raise babies, so there are all sorts of hormones that make us feel good in the direction of propagation. Some of us are obsessed with sex. These days, I'm mostly obsessed with bears. Did you know, when male bears come out of hibernation, as hungry as they are, they won't eat? They're just looking for a female, and so they spend all their time chasing them around. And in order to take care of their babies, the females just eat like crazy. Their greed for food is endless. Eventually, the male bears also need to fatten up so they can hibernate and go through the whole thing again.

So, we've got these hormones that make us pursue what feels good. They take us over. All we want is that good feeling. But we're not always aware that we're under that spell. We're just consumed by craving. Working with this Precept helps us be aware of how that greed creates harm for myself and others. And our practice of seeing the emptiness of all things, letting go of attachments for the sake of ourselves and others, includes letting go of that need for feeling good. We are able to be right here, and face whatever is present.

Fall is here. The leaves and flowers are withering. Everything starts looking a little used. Can we just be that—just be our life as it is? Can we manage our greed, anger and ignorance, and accept our life as it is? And can we, as this Precept says, " . . . embrace all experience

PRECEPT BEINGS

directly... cultivate a mind that sees clearly?" It comes off the tongue easily, but it's hard to personally and directly embrace the suffering of the world, our own suffering, trauma, neuroses and fear. The Precepts are like our guides on the path of that embrace. They are like little beings that encourage us, "Enough chocolate, Seisen. What's going on? What are you afraid of? What don't you want to face?" This awareness is the life of the Bodhisattva. Though, there's nothing necessarily Buddhist about Precept practice. Many of you aren't Buddhists, but you care deeply about embracing your life fully, being intimate with your life, as it is.

One of my biggest regrets is that somehow, I got it into my head that being in lots of physical pain while doing zazen was good, as if that was the best way to face myself directly. And there were times when *samadhi*, or whatever, would make the pain go away for a moment. But mostly, it just got worse, because the body was saying, "Don't sit like that. It hurts." I misinterpreted what that pain indicated. I thought I could just stretch my tendon and it would get better. But really, a lot of that pain is old trauma that I'm carrying around in my body. And egging it on is not the best way to work with it. So, I don't recommend sitting with intense pain. A little pain or discomfort is good. Sit in it, see what it is, who's it is. But nowadays, I'm a fan of sitting reasonably comfortably, because our stuff will still come up, regardless.

We still must open up to the painful stuff that comes up—be it emotional, physical, spiritual, whatever. That's our practice, especially during sesshin, when there's nothing else going on. It's a chance to pour our entire selves into "embrace all experience directly." Whatever comes up—I want some chocolate, I need a drink, I love meditating, I hate meditating—just watch how it comes up. I think it was Roshi Egyoku who said that Zen practice is bearing witness to pain and delusion. The delusion is that we're separate. When we really embody no-separation, the pain does disappear, because there's no one for the pain to happen to. And when you see that oneness for yourself, stay vigilant and watch all the delusions that come up around *that* experience. Notice all the ideas you have about it. Then of course, two minutes later, watch how they change.

Bodhidharma's expression of this 5th Precept says:

Self-nature is inconceivably wondrous.

He starts all of his Precept statements like that, because we think we know who we are. We get stuck on our ideas of who we are. But we are actually inconceivably wonderous—unknown and unbound.

In the intrinsically pure Dharma, not allowing the mind to become dark is called the Precept of refraining from using intoxicants.

Sometimes I use the word "dark" to refer to all the stuff we're hiding from. In that sense, going into the dark places is a good thing, because that's how we transform those dark places. But here, Bodhidharma is talking about not shutting down. We want to shine a

PRECEPT BEINGS

light on the dark places, so don't let delusions snuff out your mind's light. Not allowing the mind to shut down is at the heart of practice with this Precept.

Dogen Zenji's expression of this Precept says,

Do not introduce intoxicants. Do not make others defile themselves. This is the great awareness.

It's very important to talk about intoxicants and the dangers of drugs and alcohol. The way I am talking about this Precept is the way Maezumi Roshi did. And of course, as you know, he struggled with this relationship to alcohol. But I do think that understanding "intoxicants" to include the broader delusion of self is a more thorough way to understand this. "Do not introduce intoxicants," and then, "do not make others defile themselves". If you preach hatred and separation, or if you preach about finding your bliss and ignoring the news of the world, you're not only deluding yourself, you're encouraging others to defile themselves. That's why Right Speech is so important.

Of course, we all struggle with following the Precepts. Precept practice is not at all about becoming some kind of robot do-gooder. It's about being complicated and mysterious, allowing those little Precept beings to pop up and go, "Watch your step!" They're like little markers on the trail, and it's a rough one.

But these markers aren't always reliable. The way we study the Precepts, there are three different perspectives of each one. And no one perspective should be more highly prized than another. Sometimes, relief is desperately needed, and sharing delusion might actually be good. It could be sharing a bottle of wine with your enemy, so you can both let go of inhibitions and really speak the truth that engenders healing. That might be real medicine in the moment. In that case, using intoxicants *is* the right thing to do. When you're lost in the mountains with a bunch of bears, a cup of coffee can really do a lot of good.

These little Precept beings are always changing, in accord with everything. So, I hope you take this one of *Not Being Deluded* with you, and pay attention as it offers guidance in each moment. And never get stuck in shame or blame when you can't really understand or follow what the Precept being is telling you. The conversation will continue. All you have to do is listen.

THE BATH PATH II

We just finished the communication workshop and I wanted to do this talk in case there was something I forgot or wanted to touch on. And sure enough, a few things have come up.

We talked about how the oneness and the manyness are one. At least that's what Buddha and the Ancestors all found out. And it's something you may have experienced or you probably will experience in Zen practice, the oneness of everything. And at the same time, we're all completely unique. We have unique karma, unique lives. And those karmas are the timeless building up of ideas and concepts, both conscious and subconscious—white people are the best people, education is essential to be a good person, we should always just be having fun, we should always be working—you know, whatever we've built up and been conditioned to believe. This is the uniqueness of our very life, our path, which is unique for all of us.

One thing I stressed in the workshop is that every communication is unique. There are all kinds of communication techniques, and we went over a bunch of them.

FULL CIRCLE

When we're communicating with each other, it's always unique. So there isn't one right way of communicating—always be nice, always make strong boundaries. There isn't one rule that fits all communication. But the theory is that it is possible to connect as one in communication. And I believe most of us experience it. Sex is one way we experience that connection. Also, dancing at a concert. I've been to some great concerts where everybody's just with the music, maybe thousands of people. Like, I heard they detected a seismic shift during the Taylor Swift concert, because everybody stomped at the same moment. It's that experience of oneness while chanting during the service, or watching a great movie with a captivated audience. Oh, remember Star Wars, those of you my age? Wow, that was great. And we all were just raptured.

So, this koan I wanted to talk about is about 16 Bodhisattvas.

In the old days, there were 16 Bodhisattvas, they all got into the bath together and realized the cause of water. They called out. "This subtle touch reveals the light that is everything. We have reached the place where the sons and daughters of the Buddha Live."

This is an old story. The commentary says this probably was around the Ganges, in India. Very, very hot. And the Ganges is sacred. And so these 16 Bodhisattvas got in the river together, and the river is shallow enough that you can sit in it, and it's not too cold. It's just, wow,

THE BATH PATH II

that experience of just pure joy. So that really just shows that we can do this! We can connect with each other. And even though we're very different and we have a lot of neuroses, we can have moments of true connection. And a major part of enlightenment is practicing as a sangha—as a community—to experience this.

The 16 Bodhisattvas, by the way, are supposedly from the Diamond Realms. This is really Tibetan Buddhism, they are part of the Diamond Realm Mandala, associated with the cardinal directions, the metaphysical space inhabited by the Five Tathagatas. This relates to the Five Budda Families, which I'm going to talk about next as we publish our Sangha Sutra. The five families contain everything. They are the place where the sons and daughters of the Buddha live. And who are they? That's you, me. And I don't know how you think of Buddha. You might think, "I don't really care to be a child of Buddha." But the one that is God, oneness, whatever spirit, whatever you see as ultimate and absolute, we are their sons and daughters. And we, just like all kids, go off in our own ways. And yet still we have that oneness.

So, we've been talking a lot about the Sangha Sutra, which just came out, and it lays out in detail the Sweetwater Zen Center grievance procedure. But it's way more than that. It is really a structure for how to live together in harmony—which doesn't mean just be nicey nice. Yuck. Please, spare me. It means being authentic and truthful.

Is it true? Is it necessary? Is it kind? And is it timely? Authentic communication does not mean unfiltered communication. Please underline that. Sometimes, we should keep those harsh, mean thoughts to ourselves. Just let them go. So, is it timely? Is it true? Sometimes we have to set boundaries and be strict. But be kind.

I think about the Dalai Lama, who actually is quite fierce in his temple where he's the head person. But generally, he's so sweet and connects with everyone. I once went to this huge event with him. It was in a gym, like the Lakers gym or something. It was huge—thousands of people. And every last person I talked to said, "Oh, he looked at me, I saw him look at me!" Everybody had that experience. I did. He *was* actually looking at me. It was truly amazing, his ability to connect with everyone in that huge room. And my neighbor told me, "I saw the Dalai Lama in the Whole Foods, somewhere up north." And I said, "I completely believe you!" Because he would do that. He'd go, "I wanna see what's in this grocery store."

There's a story too about Suzuki Roshi. He had an attendant, and they were driving back from Tassajara to San Francisco and stopped at a little food place. Suzuki Roshi was vegan, and the attendant got a hamburger and he got whatever, a salad or something, and he looked at the hamburger and said, "I want that." And he and the attendant switched meals. I love that story. I'll have that hamburger. This may be breaking a boundary, and that's the other thing I wanted to talk about.

My dear friend Michael O'Keefe just published in Tricycle Magazine an article about his relationship with Roshi Bernie, who was my teacher. Michael is kind of a movie star, and he got a job on the show "Roseanne."

THE BATH PATH II

He was Roseanne's sister's boyfriend for a season or a couple seasons. He played the dumb blonde, but he made a lot of money. And Bernie kept asking him for money for his project in Yonkers, which was amazing—housing the unsheltered, education for inner city kids, hospice for people with AIDS—all of these wonderful programs. But Bernie did a lot of fundraising with Michael, and ultimately asked him for $50,000, which Michael happily gave him. And then, Bernie abruptly decided to do something else, which was Bernie's style. So, he sold everything and moved on. And I know Bernie's reasoning—it was too much for him to do at that point.

And now, the school is gone and the housing is gone. A lot of the projects that Michael donated for are just gone. The healthcare is still there and the bakery is really thriving though. They offer jobs to anyone who can lift at least 50 pounds, no background check. So, they get a lot of folks out of prison, they do training, it's a great program. But, understandably, Michael felt upset that he gave all this money for the project and Bernie just left it behind. And he wanted his money back. The whole story is in Tricycle. You can read it. Bernie pointed to what he was doing after the Yonkers project, and he said, "Well, your money's here now, wrapped up in what I'm doing now. I don't have it."

And that happened with a bunch of people. They gave their retirement money on these loans, and Bernie took a long time to pay it back, or never did. So, Bernie had problems with money. And Michael feels this was an unethical use of his money. And, it's standard fundraising. Our fundraising circle does such a good job. But I always tell the steward of the fundraising circle and the board of directors—when we raise money for a project, we have to spend that money for that project. This year we raised money around more staffing, and ended up raising more than we actually had hoped to get. And all that money has to go for staff, which is no problem because the staff is pretty expensive. Not that they get great salaries, it's just expensive for us.

The point is, this problematic power stuff is happening. In the Sangha Sutra we talk about Maezumi Roshi's difficulty with alcoholism. He would rage, he would get drunk and rage and be very inappropriate. He was a lonely man. And he had several inappropriate relationships with students. The Sangha Sutra goes into how it's egregious power abuse for teachers to have sexual relationships with students. And that's our story. That's our ancestor. That's a foundational story of the White Plum Asanga. And I've got my problems too. We all do. Everyone has stuff—neuroses, greed, anger, ignorance.

So, this moment of oneness that happens individually can also happen as a group, like with the 16 Bodhisattvas. It happens, though it is momentary and fleeting. And then we're still dealing with our greed, anger, ignorance. So, the Sangha Sutra praises the Sangha as an enlightened place, no matter who is in it. Enlightened means without greed, anger; without our egos getting messed up in it all the time. But of course they do. So that's why we have policies and guidelines. That's why we have the Precepts. Like I always say, "Red flag!" That's how I practice: red flag! We get caught up in whatever it is, and it just feels right. I had trouble with sex too.

THE BATH PATH II

Fortunately, it was before I became a teacher. At the time, it just feels like, "This is what God wants." It just feels so right, those hormones. So, to have that little Precept going, "Red flag!"

Also, the Sangha Sutra gives us information about transference, which I didn't talk about yesterday. I talked a little bit about projection. Projection is when I project my stuff on you. So if I'm lonely, I think you're lonely. And I think, "Wow, we could fix that." If I am afraid, I think you're afraid. I find myself doing that often in *dokusan*. I'll be telling someone, "You should watch out for this and that." And afterwards, I realize I was just talking to myself. It's so weird how that works. So, when relationships are difficult, well, what's the projection here? Am I projecting my desire for everything to be neat and tidy on you? You may not have that. And then transference is when I see someone else in you. One time, there was this woman who I was working with, and I just didn't like her, for no reason at all. And it was very upsetting for me. And Jikyo Roshi said, "Okay, think about her, then close your eyes . . . who comes up?" My mom's face was just, bam, right there. And I hadn't for a moment thought this was about my mom.

This is a great technique when you're having trouble and you think there might be transference going on. Werner Earhart suggested that every man is your father, every woman is your mother. And there's some truth to that. We'll project our parents onto each other, and so we just have to be aware and try to see each other authentically. Then countertransference is when the other person plays along. So if I see you as my mom, and then you start scolding me for not doing the dishes, you know, we really got ourself in a transference, countertransference. So when I say be genuinely yourself, also open up to see others genuinely, who they really are.

Many of the White Plum teachers, women included, had difficulty with sexual relations with their students. I remember the first time I taught the introduction to Zen class at ZCLA, and there was a young man who just loved me, and he was very attractive. I wasn't particularly attractive to attractive men. So I was like, "This is great!" But I did call Jikyo about it, and she said, "Step back, stop what you're doing." This is going to keep on happening because the power differential—which is also addressed in the Sangha Sutra—is so attractive and makes it so easy for the student to transfer romantic partner onto a teacher, or leader. And then countertransference is when the teacher goes along with it.

This is what I wanted to tell you about. I hate talking about transference and countertransference, but it's caused so much harm in our lineage in many different ways. Rinzai talked about it in the *Rinzairoku*, which is from China, before Dogen. He says it's like the student has a tray, a lacquer tray that's just been painted. So it's all wet and sticky. That's the student presenting with their stuff, their stuck places. The teacher sees it and jumps on it in joy and enthusiasm and gets stuck in the lacquer. Transference, countertransference right there. I love that analogy. I'll have to talk about the *Rinzairoku* sometime. He talks a lot about the teacher-student relationship.

Since seeing Michael's article, I thought I'd talk a little bit about the shadow of our lineage and how projection, transference and countertransference are part of the ways that we look at the greed, anger and ignorance that we're all working with. And that's why we have trouble connecting—our "stuff" gets in the way. That's also why it's great to do Zen together, you really can experience that oneness, sitting together. And then working together, doing service together—wonderful ways to work on appropriate relations. I mean, really, truly loving relations. Truly loving relations means I want to take care of you. So if somebody says, "I want my money back," you say, "Okay, here you go." Maybe, or maybe you don't. But to approach it with kindness, appropriateness, timeliness in our interactions.

EVERY DAY IS TRUE NATURE

We just finished a short sesshin, and those of us who participated are feeling a little tired and ready to go do something else. Sesshin is an amazing practice, and I always forget that. I've done hundreds of sesshins and I always forget how profound it is—and also how tiring it can be.

What I want to talk about is the sixth case of *The Blue Cliff Record*, but we also see it in a slightly different form earlier in koan study. It shows up in the 200 Dharmakaya Koans, and I want to discuss that version:

> *Uman introduced the subject saying, "I do not ask you about 15 days ago. What about 15 days hence? Come say a word about this." He himself replied for them, "Every day is a good day."*

This is quoted fairly often. I mean, "It's all good." We hear that a lot.

The dedication today during service, (our dedication is getting longer and longer), it was to ending systemic racism, and to all of those suffering through the pandemic. Which is all of us, right? Oh, and also for an end to the conflict in Ukraine. So, there's so much suffering going on. And I don't know if these days are unusual or if it's always been this way. I just read that now they're going into Kiev and finding horrible things and, really, genocide. I guess when you kill the people who aren't soldiers—the workers and families and children—that's genocide. That's a war crime. And, that's happened forever. The Europeans came to the land that we call the United States now and practiced genocide. The Holocaust. It seems like since mankind started . . . I mean, who takes care of their problems by killing each other? We learn when we're three that that's not the solution. But somehow we do that. We do that.

We hate based on color, different cultural practices, anything different from ourselves. Somehow, hatred is something that comes easily to us. And even if we fixed our greed, anger, and ignorance, if we were able to fix our human failings, we're still stuck with natural disasters like pandemics and tsunamis. So there's a lot of suffering going on. And actually, that's what Buddha said. The First Noble Truth is: life is suffering. We don't get what we want, and we get what we don't want.

So what does this mean, "Every day is a good day?" He certainly can't be saying that all the suffering that happens is good—that the pain we have in our lives is good. What is he talking about? Of course, he's talking about what Buddha found out: waking up to our true nature. Which is beyond human, beyond suffering and joy. It's bigger than human; it holds everything.

EVERY DAY IS TRUE NATURE

Everything is included. True nature is perfect, all complete. And the various aspects of our lives are teeny compared to the wonder of the absolute, true self.

So, when he says, "Every day's a good day," he's referring to the fact that every moment is that very same true nature. Every moment is infinite in all directions, contains everything, includes everyone. And what he's encouraging all of us to do is realize that. Which, of course, we all can. Buddha wasn't special. I guess he was kind of a prince or something in India, but he was human just like all of us. True nature is simply what each of us is. The only thing that stops any of us from manifesting that is our set of ideas and concepts. That's the second Noble Truth: there's a reason we don't see our true nature. And that reason is our upside-down thinking. We identify with this little aggregate of karma that suffers. But we have a way out of that attachment. That's the third Noble Truth: there's an end to suffering. And there's a way to do that—The Eightfold Path—which, of course, is the fourth Noble Truth. And the Eightfold Path is generally to just be a good person. We might say it's following the Precepts.

Do meditation; realize the oneness of all things; experience *samadhi*. Meditation takes effort—showing up on Sunday morning and sitting with the sangha, showing up for morning sitting. It takes effort. And this effort is, of course, effortless. Because once you wake up, you see you never needed to do anything at all. But part of that Eightfold Path is Right Effort.

And then there's Right Mindfulness, which is just paying attention to this. So, in the koan, Uman is talking about mindfulness, in a way. What about this? What about right now? It's cloudy here, and the dogs, Bruno and Chanel, are just staring.

So right now, what's going on? That's mindfulness. And then there's Right Concentration. That's the *samadhi*, the concentration. When we practice zazen—being one with this moment, following the breath, sitting with koans—at some point something shifts and we have some *samadhi* experience. No-self, emptiness. I see first hand that my life and my suffering are empty, that they don't exist. That's the immense power of zazen. But it's all about living our life intent on realizing this for ourselves and manifesting it for others. So, living a spiritual path, essentially, is our vow. And there are many, many different spiritual paths. Ultimately, it's incumbent upon us to choose one and do that.

And then there's Right View, which is seeing what our life really is. Part of that is realizing the oneness of all things. So, the right view is seeing the oneness of all things; however it's also seeing the differences. That's the Three Treasures: Buddha, Dharma and Sangha. Buddha is the oneness of all things—"every day is a good day." Dharma is everything in our life, all the differences. That includes racism, pandemic and war. It includes everything. A lot of which is difficult stuff. And Sangha is the deep harmony between the oneness and the differences. So, to say, "Every day is a good day," is to say that in the midst of our intricate lives, we can have that realization of the perfection of wisdom.

No matter how difficult our life becomes, we also know it's empty. We know it's immortal. We know it is

EVERY DAY IS TRUE NATURE

one. Buddha and Dharma work together. Master Dogen says, when you see one side, you don't see the other side. Sometimes we're in a deep *samadhi* and everything's just perfect, it's so blissful. And sometimes we're aware of the terrible suffering of the world, which is all my suffering. Sometimes, it's my irritation. And at the same time, it's perfect.

Back to the koan—what about the past? What about the future? What he's saying is, when we're meditating, just be here. Let go of the guilt, the grief, the nostalgia, all the stuff we put together from the past. Let go of that and be here.

And of course, that doesn't mean we should disregard history. History is part of here. So, when we look at how we behave, let's learn from the terrible things that have happened, and let's tell the truth about what's happened. That's why it is so important to tell the truth and not repeat history. The same goes for the future. Let go of planning, figuring out how it could be better, what I need to do to make it better. Let go of all of that. And at the same time, of course, it's good to plan. Of course, we need to plan our lives and decide how we're going to do things. But in zazen, for just this moment, what happens if you just let go? This is a perfect little instruction on how to do zazen: let go of the past, let go of the future, just be here. And then you'll realize what this "every day is a good day" is.

PICNIC ZEN

I found this website, which is called "Hotetsu's Zen Blog." It's by this guy named Meredith Hotetsu Garmon, who has practiced with many teachers. But this Zen blog is so wonderful because he gives great commentary on koans. Of course, everybody likes to talk about their ideas about koans, but he has compiled many different translations and commentaries. It's a great resource. And I used it for this talk.

This koan is from the *Blue Cliff Record* and is about a Chinese Zen teacher named Changsha. The Japanese is Chosha, but Changsha is his Chinese name.

> Changsha one day went on a picnic in the mountains. When he returned to the gate, the head monk asked, "Your reverence, where have you been wandering?" Changsha said, "I have come from strolling in the hills." The head monk said, "Where did you go?" He said, "I went following the scented grasses. Then I came back following the falling flowers." The head monk said, "That's spring mood itself."

FULL CIRCLE

Changsha says, "Well, it's better than the Autumn dew falling on the lotus flowers." Setcho commented, "I am grateful for that answer."

This is a koan that's been on my mind so much. In my recent travels, I fell in love with Denali Wilderness Park. I'd never been in such expansive wilderness. When I was there, I thought about this koan a lot. In the blog about this koan, Aitken Roshi says, "This is one of the most important koans besides *mu*," which is often a student's first koan. What is Buddha Nature? *Mu*, empty. What does that mean? What is that? I'm sure all of you right now are thinking things about what it means. But it's not about thinking in the way we usually think of thinking. Dogen said, "Think of non-thinking." That's maybe one of the deepest koans. What does that mean? How do we use our mind non-dually?

There are so many levels to each koan. You can approach them from so many different angles, and there are always aspects we still don't quite get. That's the power of koan. And that's why they've lasted for hundreds, even thousands of years. There's so much; they're so rich. You can sit with one koan forever. There are always more nuances, and this one's very nuanced.

The head monk in the story is kind of like the person in charge of training at the temple. He's the training master or something like that, which I think is better for this koan. "Head monk" is more like a temporary position during an ango, or intensive practice period, and someone takes on that role for that time. It's kind of a junior position. In some ways it's senior—usually

PICNIC ZEN

you have to sit with a sangha for quite a while before being named *shuso* or head monk for an ango. And it's a practitioner's first time taking the responsibility of a senior student. But calling this guy in the koan the person in charge of training makes more sense. But we can just call him—or her—"head monk." They certainly could have been a woman passing as a man in order to practice. I'm sure there are tons of untold stories like that.

So, the head monk sees the abbot (Changsha) coming in from a stroll. Well, this is the only translation I've seen that says he went on a "picnic", which I like because it conveys the right flavor. And maybe he had a couple of rice balls in his pocket. But essentially, he went for a walk in the mountains. He comes back and the head monk says, "Your reverence, where have you been wandering?" The way I see it, this head monk is actually a little miffed. He's there taking care of everything—getting up early, maybe something like 3:30am, and working all day to make sure everything is operating. When I was in Japan we got up at 3:30am to do yoga before sitting, which was at 4:30, I think. But anyway, they're all getting up very early, they're sitting, and they're working very hard all day. They're doing service. It's a difficult, disciplined life to do Zen practice.

Some of you are finishing ango soon. Some of you have been following the full schedule, and I know you're tired and cranky. It is hard to commit to the schedule. Oftentimes you just don't want to. When I was at Zuiō-ji in Japan, I was doing very hard, traditional practice with Enkyo Roshi. Oh my goodness, we got so cranky. We shared a room, and we drew a line down the middle of the floor, to separate my side and her side. We were cranky. Enkyo accused me of taking her towel. So, I grabbed my towel and put "Seisen" on it with a marker. She's my dearest friend, but that was hard.

So, we had a calendar. We marked off every day that passed, and we did it as a ceremony. It was so hard. And I remember saying, "we're going to remember this as a great experience." But man, I was in such pain. And we would sit with no cushions, by the way, just straight on the tatami. I had terrible wounds on my legs, wrapped in bandages. It was so challenging to practice there, and eventually, I just broke. And it wasn't like some blissful, rainbows and unicorns enlightenment. I broke. It was tough enough, and in the right way, that I finally let go. That's what that kind of training is about. And there are no words to describe how powerful it is as a spiritual practice. There are other spiritual practices, and they work great too, I'm sure. This is just mine.

So, that's where the head monk's coming from. And here's the abbot, having a blast, wandering through the mountains. That's why I'm getting that the head monk is a little annoyed. And he says, "Where have you been?" The commentary says this is kind of a Dharma challenge. I'm not into Dharma combat these days. We do enough Dharma combat in our lives, trying to get along together. So, I'm not into trying to poke people and figuring out cool Zen things to say, which can be very passive-aggressive, a way to put people down. So, I'm not a big advocate of it. But these guys, our ancestors, cultivated that kind of expression. So, let's say the head monk's poking him. "Where have you been?"

PICNIC ZEN

Which could really be, "Here I am holding down this really tough practice and serving as the example and encouraging people to do it. And you're off following butterflies!" Where have you been? Where are you? Is there anywhere to go? There's also that flavor here—investigate where we're going, what we're going to do next, what we're planning.

And Changsha just answers simply. He's not falling into some Dharma combat thing either. "I have come from strolling in the hills," I went for a little walk. And again, the head monk pokes, "Where did you go?" It's like he's baiting Changsha to name a place so that he can respond by saying something Zenny—"every place is here" or something.

There's that one koan where The Buddha says, "This would be a good place for a temple." Then Indra takes a piece of grass, places it there and says, "The Temple has been built." And it's true. At all times, just this is a good place for a temple. Intrinsically, even a place like present day Gaza, with bombs raining down, is a good place for a temple. How can we truly, really experience that *everywhere* is holy, sacred, enlightened?

So, "Where did you go?" And Changsha the abbot says, "I went following the scented grasses, then came back following the following flowers." Here is where we start to get a sense of the theme of this koan. Our head monk, as we've seen, is hinting towards the oneness, the perfection of just this moment, the experience of no-self. And that comes from concentrated sitting, from doing ango. It's that experience of letting go—of attachments, of pain and also joy. It's just being this moment, and everything is essentially perfect. This could be called the *absolute* experience. And it's crucial in Zen practice to experience that. So, the head monk is presenting that.

The abbot is representing our karmic life that all of us are living. There *is* cruelty and suffering—killing each other, throwing rockets at each other. We used to have rock fights when I was a kid. I don't know if the kids still do that. Our parents obviously didn't know, but there would be a vacant lot and we'd go throw rocks at each other. Why? Why do we do that? It hurts when you get hit with a rock. But our karma gives us circumstances, sometimes painful ones, that make us invite pain.

Changsha's response sounds like a cheerful thing, "I went following the scented grasses and came back following the falling flowers." It's like when we're young and everything's full of hope and flowers, and we have this exciting, long journey in front of us. And we really believe that we can make peace, take care of the environment, have the perfect relationship, and get whatever career we want. We follow those scented grasses, and then come back following the falling flowers. As we age, some of those hopes and dreams die. We don't end war. We don't fix the planet. Our partners and kids are flawed and do what they want to do. And then we face death.

From that perspective he's referring to our karmic conditions. Our karma arises out of the oneness, the emptiness that the head monk was nodding to. Karma's a bitch. But the only way we can know for ourselves freedom from karma is through deep intimacy with it.

Intensive zazen practice, like sesshin and ango, is essential on the Zen path. Zen *means* meditation. But we

PICNIC ZEN

also have to devote ourselves to our life practice, Precept practice. I hope you are inspired to at some point. Sit until it sucks, and then sit a little more. And engage in your life in the same way, with the same intention.

I recently read a book that addresses mental illness. Its basic point is that you have to go into the abyss. The protagonist doesn't find sanity, per se, but he figures out how to accept and live with who he is. The way he finds that peace is by going to the depths of his fear, of his disappointment. And in the book, when you penetrate the abyss, it's actually full of treasure. So our protagonist grabs all this treasure from his abyss and he takes it with him. But as soon as he starts to leave, the treasure just vanishes into vapor. And he realizes—oh, that abyss is always there. That's like our practice. We put forth so much effort to get to the bottom of it, of this, of us. That's why it's so hard to sit. You bump into all the stuff you don't want to look at: fear, guilt, physical pain. It's very hard to be with our abyss. So, the power of relying on the schedule allows us to just keep going, searching for the treasure in the abyss. Of course, you can say "uncle," you can walk away anytime when it really doesn't feel safe. But having that vow to wake up, stay with it.

At the end of this sesshin coming up, Kyoshin's going to receive lay Denkai, which we call Preceptor transmission. The Precepts guide us in living our karmic life from the standpoint of emptiness, or awakening. It's not either/or the head monk's point of view, or the abbot's. We can be stuck in enlightenment, full of "everything's fine as it is." And we can get stuck in the heaviness of karma. The truth is, they are one, they work together. The Precepts are guidelines on how to navigate life and our karma. Don't lie, don't steal, etc. And, of course, we all can't help but continue to do that stuff. Maybe you don't, but I do. The Precepts are continuous practice. Just like sitting with oneness is continuous practice. Notice, "Wow, I just lied. Why did I do that?" Dig into the Precepts and dig into your life, which is following the grasses and the falling flowers.

The head monk in the koan is intent on doing Dharma combat. So, he continues saying, "That is spring mood itself." He's also still mad at the abbot for going on a picnic in the middle of ango. So, his statement has a little feeling of—aren't you special? La-di-da! And Changsha says, "It's better than the Autumn Dew falling on the lotus flowers." Even better than living in emptiness and no-self is getting to know your life, with all its ups and downs, as not separate from that emptiness.

Sekiso comments, "Changsha has walked wholeheartedly in the grass." He's totally one with his life. And of course we don't do that. We're always whining. Well, maybe you're not, but I am always whining that it could have been better. Why did that happen to me? It's not fair. There's too much grief. So, instead of whining and judging and comparing, live wholeheartedly. I've been practicing that while driving to the border, because it is never a smooth experience. One time, it was the day of the races in Ensenada, and the whole city was just so crowded and full of people. And I was so annoyed, "I have to get to the Zendo on time to be holy!" But then I really focused on being wholly present and I

PICNIC ZEN

started watching the crowds. The crowds at the races are wonderful, so much to see and take in. I'm so glad my attention went to that instead of my whining. How can we better accept our life and do what we can to make it better? Accepting doesn't mean we never take action. We can accept and then do what we can to limit suffering for ourselves and others.

Another comment from the blog says, "Changsha is sitting in a forest of thorns," which is our life—sitting in a forest of thorns. What frees us from it is the realization of no-self, of just this as perfect. That realization helps us practice the Precepts so we don't get pricked too often, as we follow scented grasses and falling flowers.

ON RELATIONSHIP I

Thank you for your practice. I can feel it here in Baja. It's in the air everywhere here, your practice. And I want to encourage you to stay with it, to keep on going.

I saw this thing Tricycle Magazine sent out—two essays on practicing with relationship. And it caught my eye because I think I've always thought that Zen practice is a solitary sport, which is weird because it's obviously not. But somehow, in my mind, good Zen practice looked like sitting by yourself and waking up to this moment. Even if we don't have all the things we want, our life is perfect, whole, complete, and there's great joy in every moment of life. See that for yourself. It sounds like a solo activity.

In a way, it's true that traditional Zen practice, maybe back in Dogen Zenji's time, and even to some degree now, was mostly for people who were single, or celibate. And I just always had that image of sitting alone somewhere on a mountain top. But in fact, one of the Three Treasures of Buddhism is the Sangha, or community. The Three Treasures are Buddha, Dharma and Sangha.

Buddha is awakening to the fact that as it is, this moment is one with everything. Dharma is the teachings of the Buddha, and the Sangha is the people you practice with.

The Sangha Treasure can be seen on so many different levels. Our sangha is the people in our community, the people in our neighborhood, our country. It's the animals and plants we share this planet with. But generally, we can say for sure that one of the Three Treasures is about practicing together and being in relationship.

I like the first part of *The Three Pillars of Zen*, Yasutani Roshi's instructions for how to do zazen. He tried to write for Westerners, and it's very handy if you're starting on your Zen path. It's not very long, but it has everything in there—kinhin and sitting—and it describes five different reasons to practice. Each of us has a unique practice path. Picture a forest. We each walk through that forest, dodging rocks, hopping over tree stumps, finding our own way to become enlightened. There's no ultimate or best path. There's just the forest. There's no pre-determined path for anybody. And of course, the forest itself is the enlightenment; there's nowhere to get to.

However, every once in a while, we feel like we're lost, like we've lost some kind of path we were on. But really, we can wake up to the reality that whatever we're doing, wherever we're going is undoubtedly enlightenment itself. Whatever reasons you have for doing Zen practice are uniquely your own, and there's no need to compare them to anyone else's. And when we share ourselves with our sangha, we find out that we all have different reasons, different expectations, different paths. And that's such a beautiful way to connect with each other.

ON RELATIONSHIP I

The five reasons to practice that Yasutani Roshi lays out are in some kind of order, though I'm sure there's no meaning or value to the order. The first reason to practice is about physical and mental wellbeing. Nowadays, meditation is recommended for just about anything. The power of meditation for health and wellbeing is tremendous. For many of us, that's what brings us to practice—a health issue, emotional issues, etc. We want to heal and feel better, so we turn to meditation.

The second reason is the "Outside Way," which is like Bernie's successor Father Kennedy. He was a serious Zen practitioner, a wonderful Zen master, but primarily a Catholic priest. He wasn't a Buddhist, but he wanted to supplement his faith with meditation practice. The third reason is simply to get enlightened, to have the same experience the Buddha had under the Bodhi Tree. Fourth is practicing with the Bodhisattva vow, which is to live an enlightened life by serving others in whatever way I can. And finally, the fifth reason is what we call *shikantaza*[6] which is just this. No reason, no concept of reason. That's why I practice.

But I've been really aware recently that this list of reasons doesn't mention relationship. What about practicing for the sake of healthy, deeply connected relationship? So I wanted to read you some stuff from the Tricycle articles I mentioned. One of the writers is Norman Fischer, who is a wonderful Zen master in Suzuki Roshi's lineage. He says:

> *We're not anyone in particular. Every moment, in response to the conditions in front of us, another*

person, the sky, the flowers, we are created again. That's who we are, our relationship in this moment. Of course, conventionally, we have identities, commitments, loves, hates, and preferences. But that's not all of who we are. That's the point of Zen practice. And I think of all spiritual practice: to get in touch with the person that we are beyond the person we seem to be.

We don't really ever come to that understanding and realization by ourselves. In Zen practice, it is understood that we enact this wisdom in our connection to one another. It's our Dharma relations renewed, moment by moment, as we meet each thing and each person that brings us to the truth, and a kind of awakening within and beyond our suffering.

When you think about Zen stories, this is how they work. They are not talks given by wise teachers. They're encounters between people. Every Zen story is a story of a meeting. It's a story of a relationship. And as we see from these stories, not necessarily a conventional notion of relationship in which we're fulfilling each other's needs, but a more profound sense of our connection to one another.

When Buddha was born, he said, "Above the heavens, below the earth, I alone, the World Honored One." That doesn't mean—I'm better than everybody. It means that my true nature is everything. Each of us can say

ON RELATIONSHIP I

that. What we are is Indra's Net, interconnected with everything, which is even scientifically accurate. Every atom in the universe is connected through energy. And that connection is constantly changing and constantly moving. So, my essential nature is nothing more than relationship to everything. That's what Buddha meant in his precocious baby declaration.

I'm also reminded of the koan from the *Mumonkan* where Zuigan calls to himself.

> *Every day, Zuigan would say, "Master?" And he himself would answer, "Yes."*
>
> *"Are you in?"*
>
> *"Yes."*
>
> *"Don't be deceived by others."*

This can be seen as—don't be deceived that there's anything separate from this, separate from you. And of course, we're constantly deceived—constantly judging, constantly labeling good and bad, right and wrong. Every interaction elicits our comments and opinions.

Most of our koans are about relationship. It's often about the relationship between teacher and student. In Zen, working with a teacher is so important. The transmission of the Dharma, the Buddha Seal, comes through that teacher-student relationship. Of course, there's nothing to transmit. Here it is in front of you. But there is a unique connection and trust that is developed through that relationship. It's like that koan about the chick inside the egg. For the chick to be born and free itself from its shell, the hen pecks from the outside and the chick pecks from the inside. That shell is our stuff, our karma, our ego. Teachers have needs, and neuroses, and twisted karma just like their students do. So, we work on those together. And that connection is who we are. It applies to the whole sangha, your Dharma brothers and sisters, the people you live and practice with.

Sangha is like one of those machines that polishes rocks. You turn the handle that tosses the rocks around, and the rocks bump up against each other until they're polished. Similarly, practicing together, we polish each other. And you could say that about any group of people—a family, friends, neighbors. We have the opportunity to practice with everyone in our lives; we can practice having that experience of connection. And how to do that is by letting go of our ideas and concepts, our modes of separation.

Sometimes it feels like it's better to be single. It's better not to have a family, or neighbors. It's better to practice in a monastic setting. But let me read something from the other piece that was in Tricycle. This one is by a Tibetan teacher named Anam Thubten.

> In Tibet, a respected practitioner of Chöd was once asked if he had ever done a journey into the haunted ground of the cemetery. He said, "No, I haven't gone. I don't need to go because I'm married."

In other words, I don't need to go into haunted scary places, because I get enough scary stuff being married.

ON RELATIONSHIP I

"Within the haunted ground of relationships, many old neurotic patterns get triggered. We develop habits of dumping emotional baggage on our partners, triggering reactions that ricochet back on us when we are blind to our own demons of jealousy, complaint, paranoia, and dissatisfaction. These unresolved shadowy patterns are easily projected on the other, but they are the demons of our own unfinished issues."

He goes into detail about the difficulties that we experience in relationship. The article is mostly about romantic relationship, but I think it applies to any kind of relationship. There's the honeymoon period. It feels like you've found a soulmate, someone who really gets you and makes life easier. And it feels like life is going to be perfect from now on. Then, at some point we start triggering each other, and it becomes more like the relationship between that hen and the egg. That shell starts to get in the way, and we start getting irritated. We discover ways our values don't align. And certainly, if it's toxic, you should leave. If it's abusive, you should leave. If you've done everything you can to work on it, you should leave. But I'm so quick to write relationships off, I'm like—one trigger, I'm gone.

But I love that in this article, he says that that's the *good* part of the relationship. Difficulty and conflict create the place where you can use the relationship to work on yourself. It can help illuminate the barriers we have to waking up—our attachments to ideas and concepts. The way we separate from each other is through greed, anger, and ignorance. When I'm not getting what I want, when you're upsetting me all the time, I forget that there's no self, that we are one. Those are very powerful points of practice. That's why both of these articles are saying that relationships are good for our practice.

It can get tricky. Relationships can naturally trigger our greed and attachment, which separates us from true self. But on the other hand, love is an aspect of true self. Samantabhadra is the Bodhisattva of love. I think love is different from compassion. In compassion, there's a little bit of a power imbalance—"I care about you. I really feel your pain. I'm so sorry. I want to help you." But love is total connection; it's not transactional. Love isn't about being of service. It is ultimate equality, completely mutual vulnerability. It could be love that holds everything together in Indra's Net.

So, relationship practice is a wonderful way to look at collective awakening and the Sangha Treasure. I'm really getting to experience that now, living in community here in Baja, Mexico. Everyone is so cool and interesting, and yet, we all have so many different ideas and opinions about things. So, I've been practicing seeing everyone as Buddha, and fully appreciating everyone, just as they are. And when people are irritating me, I get to look at how that could be *my* stuff—my shell—getting in the way.

There are so many different paths for practice. And it's so silly to have an idea about the *right* way to practice. Each of us finds our own way according to our unique karma. So, I think it's important for each of us to continually clarify our vow. The ancients of our

ON RELATIONSHIP I

lineage give us wonderful examples of practice. But like Maezumi Roshi always said, "It's up to you now, how Zen is going to evolve." It's up to us, how Zen practice will be of value in our time and place. Of course, we rely on the great teachings of the past, and we honor the old monastic models appropriately. But retreating into the mountains may not be the best upaya—skillful means—for this time.

For me, it always comes back to zazen. I can't imagine a Zen path without serious zazen time. That's what I want to emphasize most: keep your zazen practice going. I know, I'm preaching to the choir, once again. And I'm so happy that that's the case. What we go through during sesshin is something I don't experience in any other context or modality. It offers a uniquely profound release of those ancient patterns that we've developed in our bodies. So, I encourage you to keep on sitting, and also to approach your relationships as a deep spiritual practice.

Even in sesshin, when you're not speaking to each other, there's still a lot of relationship practice happening. The noises people make, or people not doing their job right—even in silence there are constant opportunities to be triggered and peck at our shells. I sat with Peter Matthiessen for years, and I admired him, of course, but I never talked to him. He would come right when sesshin started and leave right when it ended. So, we never talked, but we sat together for many sesshins. And when we finally did have a conversation, it was like we were best friends. We had gone through so much together, even if it was all in silence.

FULL CIRCLE

I'm sorry I can't be there with you all the time. When this last sesshin started, I was glad I wasn't going to do the whole thing. And now, I'm jealous of those of you who are doing the whole thing, because it really is the most transformational practice I know. And I encourage you to approach your sesshin as a practice of relationship, not a practice of solitude. Allow space for love to arise in the midst of your sitting. Then, we can awaken together, as one.

ON RELATIONSHIP II

Some of us have experienced relationships as being an obstacle to serious Zen practice, whatever "serious Zen practice" means. It's hard to commit to intensive practice, *and* have a social life, *and* have a family, a partner, etc. So, I used to think about being in a relationship as a problem for Zen practice. But now it's so obvious to me that relationship is really what Zen practice is all about. Why get enlightened? So we can be in harmony with everything in our life, which is relationship.

The realization of the Buddha is the realization that all beings are one. It's a realization about relationship. The koans are pretty much about relationship, often between teacher and student. Dharma transmission is all about that relationship between teacher and student. In a way, there is nothing to transmit, because as you are is awakened. But in another way, that recognition by the teacher, "You have my mind," is how the Dharma has been passed down for thousands of years. It started with the Buddha and his successor Mahākāśyapa. It's not like an exam, like you passed the SATs. In Buddha's case, he held up a flower, and Mahākāśyapa smiled. This simple expression really clarified for the Buddha, "You have my mind. And I charge you to pass it on to others."

What is that Buddha mind? What is this true self? What is it to drop off body and mind? How do we directly experience that? And like my favorite koan, where the 16 Bodhisattvas awaken together in the bath, how do we experience True self together, as one? That's at the heart of my practice these days—collective awakening. And maybe a couple of those 16 Bodhisattvas were just pretending, to fit in with the group. It's like the green flash we have here in Baja when the sun goes down. Lots of people will pretend to see it, just to be in solidarity.

So, these Bodhisattvas file into the bath, following the rules, following the schedule, following the group. In many monasteries, the rules are very strict. Every moment you're doing something. When the bell rings to end work, for example, even if you only have one weed left, you drop what you're doing and move on to the next thing in the schedule. Sound of the bell, put it down. That's the spirit with which these Bodhisattvas file into the bath. It's not break time, it's just simply what we do now, as one. Suddenly they experience realization through the touch of the water. They experience complete freedom, total liberation, in the midst of following this rigid schedule. And they experience it together, with no separation between self and other.

The commentary on the koan says, "You'll be able to attain to this only after seven times piercing and eight times breaking through." That's our practice!

ON RELATIONSHIP II

It reminds me of this Italian movie called "Still Time." The protagonist is a workaholic, and he's filled with greed, anger, and ignorance. He's an asshole about getting ahead in his career. Basically, the premise of the movie is that he's only really present and aware on his birthday. The rest of the time he's unconscious, lost in his greed and delusion. But every birthday, he wakes up with a sense of clarity and presence. And that makes some sense—for many of us, our birthday is a day of self-reflection.

So, that reminds me of our practice and this point about "seven times piercing and eight times breaking through." And, actually, I think the movie covers seven years. Seven times he's truly awake, conscious of his true self. And then for the rest of the year, he's lost in his greed, anger, and ignorance. Oh, and they even quoted the Dalai Lama in it, which just proves that it was a Buddhist movie: "There are only two days in the year when nothing can be done. One is called yesterday and the other is called tomorrow. Today is the right day to love, believe, do, and mostly live."

So, over and over again, we must wake up and see our true self. And what comes out of that practice is our deep connection with each other. I like to be alone, but I go for walks because of my dogs. And if I'm feeling kind of down, in a little bit of a funk, seeing one of my neighbors and stopping to chat for five minutes is so refreshing, so joyful. And it's just small talk—we talk about the weather or whatever. But even just that small talk reminds me that there's something very awakening about genuinely connecting with people. They don't have to be people I'm particularly close to. Just connecting with other beings, without judgment, is a gateway to collective awakening.

So, I've really been switching from, "relationships stand in the way of practice," to, "the way to awakening is through relationship." It doesn't matter what the relationship is. If we just practice opening up to each other, we face an indisputable oneness. When I engage with someone, how am I judging or discriminating? How are my ideas and conditioning getting in the way of seeing that innate oneness? Where do I insert notions of power, and who should and does have it? That's my practice these days.

I think the underlying guideline for collective awakening is to practice kindness and compassion towards each other. And that's included in our formal practice together. We come to sesshin, we follow the schedule. We follow the guidelines and practices of our sangha. And within that structure, going through it together, we can wake up to that magical, yet ordinary, oneness. Don't get caught up in the structures or forms, thinking they're special or holy or something. Just engage with them in solidarity with your sangha, as a way of communicating with each other.

Practice opening up more and more with others. Make healthy boundaries where appropriate. But cultivate that honesty and genuine connection. We hold so much conditioning and so many patterns that have been firmly entrenched within us, and that get in the way of our connection with others. That's why it's so helpful to work with a therapist in tandem with doing

ON RELATIONSHIP II

Zen practice. Kokyo Roshi put it very well to me the other day. She said, "Everyone who does sesshin, or any intensive sitting, is going to bump into stuff that they very carefully put in a box long ago. And as a Zen teacher, I can't pretend to know how to unpack that box skillfully." So, it's really good to have a relationship with a therapist as you deepen your practice. Even if that's just through reading books, listening to podcasts, or following therapy social media profiles. That healing wisdom is all over the place these days.

Please stick with your zazen practice. It's the best thing there is for realizing your inherent connection with all beings. Practice with a group; jump into that pool together. Spend time investigating the patterns that keep us from connecting with each other. Through lots of zazen, you build up a lot of *samadhi,* or *joriki,* both of which give us the energy to break through our delusion. Don't spend your sitting time daydreaming and planning. Stay with this moment, whatever is coming up. Keep coming back to the breath. When it gets hard and you're consumed with who you need to call, all the housework that needs to be done, just come back to the breath, stay with it. When it's hard is the best part. It may seem like nothing is happening, or that your efforts aren't yielding anything. But because we are all inherently connected, your efforts on the cushion really do affect everything, absolutely everything in the universe. And the rooster next door just crowed in agreement with me. Take care and keep on going.

ON RELATIONSHIP III

I think you get the point by now—I see Zen as a practice of relationship. And most of our koans are about relationship, either between teacher and student, or groups of Dharma friends. I'm thinking today of the one about Zuigan's eyebrows. If you've been around a while, you've probably heard me talk about it, because I always talk about it at the end of ango, the annual—or biannual—3-month intensive practice period at a Zen temple. The koan is about a group of Dharma brothers at the end of their summer ango. Essentially, it's an exchange of their Zen understanding with each other. That relationship of Dharma siblings—those who practice together, which is all of us—is so central to awakening individually, and collectively. I'm not quite sure how individual and collective awakening are different, so, take that distinction very lightly.

There is a wealth of information about our neuroses and attachments that a relationship can reveal, that we wouldn't be able to access on our own. That includes the relationships that seem perfect. You complete each other's sentences, you have the same opinions and aesthetic, you stay up all night talking. And then little by little, if you really are close and intimate, you start to trigger each others' neuroses, and it may even threaten the relationship.

The spiritual practice part of this is to see what a wonderful opportunity for enlightenment exists in the conflict of our relationships. Because, as you know, when projection, triggers and shadows arise in relationships, it can be like a mirror in which we see how our little sense of self is asserted. And regarding ourselves as separate from anything else transgresses the reality of complete oneness. When we have relationship difficulty, by definition, we're acting as a separate self. And often that's a good thing. You can't communicate your needs or make healthy boundaries without acknowledging your separate, relative self. So, opening up and digging into the difficult parts of our relationships is a fundamental element of the Buddha Way, and our Bodhisattva vow.

It seems like there are very few koans about just one person. But there is one I mentioned the other day that I wanted to go into in more detail. This one also features Zuigan, whose eyebrows were in question in that other koan about the summer ango. It's called "Zuigan Calls Himself Master."

> *Every day, Master Zuigan used to call to himself, "Master," and he himself would answer, "Yes." Again, he would call, "Thoroughly awake, thoroughly awake," and he would answer, "Yes, yes."*

ON RELATIONSHIP III

"Don't be deceived by others any day or any time."

"No, no."

So who's the master? Who is Buddha? I was talking to someone recently about their Zen center's children's program. They were telling me that they play this little game with the kids: "Who is Buddha? Who is Buddha?" And then they say, "Look in the mirror! Look in the mirror! There's Buddha!!" You don't have to use the word Buddha. True self, Spirit, God—whatever word you use to capture that freedom from life and death—each of us, as we are, right now, is that. And then Zuigan says, "Don't be deceived by others." There's so much you can say about this teaching. But for now, I really want to highlight our practice of not being deceived by thinking there are others in the first place.

So, there is just one person in this koan. That person is Buddha, and that's you. And don't be deceived in thinking that the other people in your life are not you, that there's a separation between yourself and others. That's why relationship, which by definition assumes there are two or more separate people, is so useful for Zen practice. All of our relationships are practice—because every single last being is our teacher, is Buddha. People used to talk about how much they loved Maezumi Roshi. And they would say, "When he looks at me, he looks at me like I am Buddha."

This is what I'm practicing with now—seeing everyone as Buddha. But even that is not something to hold on to. Getting stuck in "everyone is Buddha" means you don't admonish bad behavior, or fight against immoral policies and conduct. From the *Absolute* standpoint, everyone is Buddha. But from the *Relative* standpoint, there is wrong action; there is justice through disavowing people or their behavior. And we practice to see for ourselves the *Absolute and Relative* realities as one—to see the person who causes me harm as Buddha, to see harm itself as Buddha. That's why approaching our relationships, and all the conflict that arises in them, as a gateway to enlightenment can lead to such deep connection and love.

So, I urge you all to come to the *zendo* with a mind of relationship, instead of a mind of doing something for yourself. It doesn't mean you have to talk to anyone or be particularly social or outgoing. But I want us all to see the power relationship and community have for helping us to see for ourselves what "not two, and not one" really means.

NOTES

DREAMY PEONIES

1. The organization of Zen teachers in the lineage started by Taizan Maezumi Roshi. It is comprised of ordained and lay successors of Maezumi Roshi, and all of their subsequent successors.

MANIFESTING THE THREE TREASURES

2. note that the word love is complicated in English. It can mean obsessive (one of the 3 poisons), and it can mean selfless love and compassion for all beings. In this case we are waking up from the swoon of attachment.

3. The culminating ceremony for a practice period's Head Trainee, whereby they officially become a senior student and give their first Dharma talk.

THE SANGHA SUTRA

https://cdn.prod.website-files.com/6514af110f62d16c3649f859/66a17a444babb85d2d5a8506_SWZC%20SANGHA%20SUTRA%202024.pdf.

THE BATH PATH I

4. The 5 aggregates of attachment in classic Buddhist teaching. The five skandhas are form, sensation, conception, volition and consciousness.

5. One-on-one meeting between student and Roshi (teacher). This practice and relationship are essential to maintaining the Zen Way.

THE DELUSION OF PRACTICE

Buswell, Robert E., and Donald S. Lopez. *The Princeton Dictionary of Buddhism*. Princeton University Press, 2014.

YOUR INGREDIENTS I

Uchiyama, Kosho. *How To Cook Your Life: From the Zen Kitchen to Enlightenment*. Boston: Shambhala Publications, 1970.

Glassman, Bernard, and Rick Fields. *Instructions To The Cook: A Zen Master's Lesson In Living A Life That Matters*. New York: Belltower, 1996.

ON RELATIONSHIP I

Kapleau, Phillip. *The Three Pillars of Zen: Teaching, Practice and Enlightenment*. New York: Anchor Books, 1989

6. A Japanese term that translates to "just sitting" and is a form of meditation in Zen Buddhism. It's a practice that involves being fully aware of one's thoughts, feelings, and surroundings without reacting to them. The goal is to directly experience reality and realize one's true nature.

Fischer, Norman. "We Are Our Relationships" *Tricycle Magazine*, October 26, 2021. https://tricycle.org/article/norman-fischer-relationships/.

Thubten, Anam. "What We Can Learn From The Haunted Ground Of Relationships." *Tricycle Magazine*, February 14th, 2022. https://tricycle.org/article/relationships-selflessness/.

ABOUT THE AUTHOR

Anne Seisen Saunders was born in Sheridan, WY on April 29, 1948. She received her BA in Biochemistry from UC Berkeley in 1970. In 1976, she started practicing Zen Buddhism formally with Taizan Maezumi, Roshi at Zen Center of Los Angeles. Soon after, she received *Tokudo*, becoming a priest in the Soto Zen Lineage, and ultimately completed her training and received *Shiho* (full Dharma transmission) from Roshi, Bernie Tetsugen Glassman in 1996.

In 1998, she became co-abbot of Yokoji Zen Mountain Center in Idyllwild, CA with then Sensei, Charles Tenshin Fletcher. A couple years later, in 2000, she left Yokoji to found Sweetwater Zen Center in National City, CA, where she served as abbot until 2025. She received *Inka* from Roshi, Bernie Glassman in 2007, and was appointed *Kokusaifukyoshi* (official Soto Zen teacher) by the Japanese Soto Headquarters in April of 2009. Seisen Roshi also served as president of the White Plum Asanga (community of Zen teachers in Taizan Maezumi, Roshi's lineage) for over a decade.

Seisen Roshi now lives in Ensenada, Mexico with her two dogs, Bruno and Chanel.

MORE ABOUT SEISEN ROSHI

Past treasurer the Kuroda Institute— http://uhpress.wordpress.com/books-in-series/kuroda-institute/

President/Secretary/Treasurer of White Plum Asanga— http://www.whiteplum.org/index.html

Member of American Zen Teachers Association— http://www.americanzenteachers.org/

Co-founder of Prison Meditation Project— http://www.prisonmeditation.org/

Board member of Xara Garden School (a charter school in San Diego)—http://www.xaraschools.org

Member of Friends of Friendship Park— http://friendshippark.org/frontpage.html

www.ingramcontent.com/pod-product-compliance
Lightning Source LLC
Chambersburg PA
CBHW052141070526
44585CB00017B/1920